ハートを掴む

ベストアイデアグラフィックス

IDEAS UNLEASHED

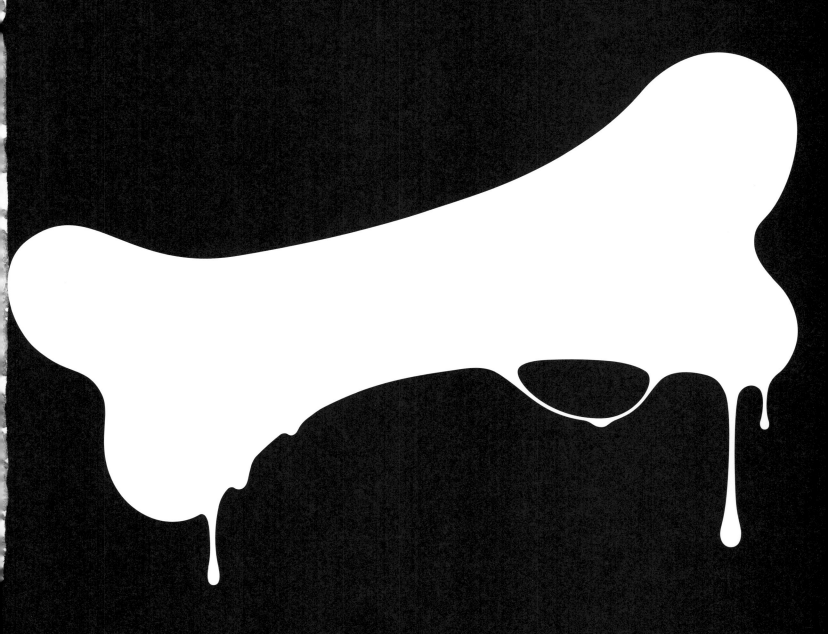

90480

Ideas Unleashed
Exceptional Achievements in Graphic Design

©2008 PIE BOOKS

PIE BOOKS
2-32-4, Minami-Otsuka, Toshima-ku, Tokyo 170-0005 Japan
tel: +81-3-5395-4811 fax: +81-3-5395-4812

e-mail: editor@piebooks.com sales@piebooks.com
http://www.piebooks.com/

ISBN978-4-89444-693-9 C3070
Printed in Japan

CONTENTS

『ハートを掴む広告とは』

広告の役割とは一体何でしょうか？
魅力的な広告とはどのようなものでしょうか？

広告の最大の役割は、商品そのものの価値やメッセージを、より多くの人々に、より広く、強く伝えることにあります。また、そのメッセージを受けとる
人々の購買意欲をかきたて、実際に購買してもらう状況にまで引き継ぐことができれば、その商品を提供する側にとってはよりよい役割を果たしている
と言えるでしょう。

広告を通して、わたしたちは商品の個性や価値を知ることができます。また、自分自身が思い込んでいた商品のイメージが、ある広告に出会うことにより
変わることもあるかもしれません。今の自分にとって本当に必要であるかをじっくり考えさせられる機会にもなるでしょう。さらには、商品を手にしたとき
の驚きや喜びの気持ちまでを連想させることで、その人と商品との距離を身近に感じさせてくれるかもしれません。つまり、商品の効果的な宣伝、プラス、
商品が取り入れられるわたしたちの日々の生活や人生を、立体的に想像させてくれることが広告の役割であると考えます。

本書では、『ハートを掴む ベストアイデアグラフィックス』と題し、デザインが魅力的なことはもちろん、広告そのものが伝えたい内容を、そのカタチや
デザインで最も効果的に落とし込んでいる作品を厳選してご紹介します。例えば、見た目のインパクトやおもしろさ、常識的なモラルを覆す発想と
意外性、フェイク、人間の視覚を刺激するカタチや印刷方法、触覚効果を狙った素材や仕掛け、コピーをじっくり眺めてみてやっとその意味が腑に落ちる、
などのアイデアコンセプトと作品説明も掲載。また、作品はキャンペーン広告からポスター、新聞広告、カタログ、ダイレクトメール、プロダクト、
ショップツール、書籍と、国内外から多種多様のラインナップが揃いました。

一般的に広告は、「一時的にわたしたちの目の前をよぎる宣伝ツール」「見る人を限定しないマスメディア」と捉えられることから、その存在は
暴力的だと言われることもしばしば。ですが、一瞬目にしただけだけれど印象深い広告、後々まで脳裏に焼きついて忘れられない広告は必ず存在して
いるはずです。短い時間でもハートを掴むことによって、人の心には一瞬ではなく永く残るものにもなりえます。

触れられるのは瞬時だけれど心のなかで永遠になりうる、そんな広告がたくさん世の中に溢れたら、その広告を見る出来る限り多くの人々がそれぞれの
立ち位置でしっかり感じたり考えたりし、世界もきっともっと楽しく充実するはずです。

この書籍をご覧いただく皆様には、作品からそんなアイデアのエッセンスを感じとっていただけたなら幸いです。

最後になりましたが、お忙しい中、アイデア溢れる貴重な作品をご提供くださいました出品者の方々へ、また制作にあたりご協力いただきました
すべての方々へ、この場をお借りして心より御礼申し上げます。

PIE BOOKS 編集部

When ideas are unleashed

Advertising – What is its real purpose?

What makes an inspirational advertisement?

Advertising's main purpose is to communicate a powerful and widespread message to as large an audience as possible about how a product is of value in our lives. For an advertiser who has a product to sell, an advertisement is considered successful if it not only stimulates a desire to purchase the product in the audience who receives the advertiser's message but also makes them go a step further and actually purchase it.

Advertising informs us about the differences between products and how a product can be of value to us. A stubborn idea we have in our mind about a certain product may change as a result of seeing an advertisement. Advertising may also present an opportunity to reconsider whether we might need a product in our lives at a certain point in time. The advertiser may create a feeling in us of accessibility to a product by connecting it to the human emotions of surprise and joy that we experience when we hold a product in our hands. In other words, it is advertising's purpose to market a product effectively and to make us imagine that product as a part of our everyday lives in some concrete way.

In this book titled "Ideas Unleashed: Exceptional Achievements in Graphic Design," we introduce a collection of advertisements selected for their inspirational design and for the way they use their form and their design to effectively incorporate the message the advertiser wants to convey. The book also contains concepts and commentary on advertising that is catchy and has visual impact, incorporates ideas that challenge accepted thinking or an element of surprise, are produced in a form and printed in a way that is visually exhilarating, use materials and mechanisms to produce a tactile effect, or make us stop and think before we are able to make sense of it. The extensive range of advertising examples includes posters, newspaper advertisements, catalogues, direct mail, campaign products, shop tools and books that were part of advertising campaigns both in Japan and the rest of the world. Because it is generally regarded as a promotional tool that flashes in front of our eyes for a few seconds or a mass medium with a limitless number of viewers, it is often commented that advertising has somewhat of a harsh nature. But advertising that makes a profound impression on us and imprints itself on the brain to become unforgettable although seen for only a matter of seconds definitely exists. Some advertising captures the human heart within a matter of seconds and is then capable of residing there forever, not just for a fleeting moment. If the world abounded in more such advertising, advertising that touches us for a moment and remains in our hearts forever, and as many people as possible saw and responded to it in their own emotional and intellectual way, the world would surely be a more joyful and satisfying place.

We would be overjoyed were the readers of this book to assimilate the essence of the ideas contained in the featured advertisements. Finally, we wish to express here our sincere appreciation to the contributors who made time in their busy lives to provide us with invaluable material for the book, material that abounds with ideas, and to all those people who contributed in the its production.

The editorial staff PIE BOOKS

エディトリアルノート
Editorial Notes

a

作品タイトル名
Title of Work

b

クライアント［業種名］
Clients [a Type of Industry]

c

制作国
Country from which submitted

d

スタッフクレジット
Staff Credit

CD＝クリエイティブ・ディレクター　Creative Director
AD＝アート・ディレクター　Art Director
D＝デザイナー　Designer
I＝イラストレーター　Illustrator
CW＝コピーライター　Copywriter
P＝フォトグラファー　Photographer
DF＝制作会社　Design Firm
SB＝作品提供社　Submittor
E-＝エグゼクティブ〜　Executive

e

デザインコンセプト
Design Concept

※上記以外の制作者呼称は省略せずに
掲載しています。
All other production titles are unabbreviated.

※本書に掲載されている店名、店舗写真、
販促ツール、商品などは、すべて
2008年6月時点での情報になります。
All in store-related information, including
shop name, photography, promotional items
and products are accurate as of June 2008.

※本書に掲載されているキャンペーン、
プロモーションは、既に終了しているものも
ありますので、ご了承ください。
Please note that some campaigns and
promotions are no longer deployed.

※作品提供者の意向によりデータの一部を
記載していない場合があります。
Please note that some credit information has
been omitted at the request of the submittor.

※各企業に附随する、〝株式会社、（株）〟
および〝有限会社、（有）〟は表記を
省略させて頂きました。
The "kabushiki gaisha (K.K.)" and "yugen
gaisha (Ltd.)" portions of all Japanese
company name have been omitted.

※本書に記載された企業名・商品名は、
掲載各社の商標または登録商標です。
The company and product names that appear
in this book are published and/or registered
trademarks.

a 〝クノールカップスープ〟つらら中吊り広告
"Knoll Cup Soup" Icicle Hunging Advertisement
b 飲食料品メーカー　Foodstuff Manufacturer ｜ Japan **c**

d CL＝味の素　AJINOMOTO CO., INC.
CD＋AD＝谷一和志　Kazushi Taniichi
D＝小塚泰彦　Yasuhiko Kozuka
D＝中島淳志　Atsushi Nakajima
CW＝小林孝悦　Takayoshi Kobayashi
P＝大手仁志　Hitoshi Ote
CG＝中島輝子　Teruko Nakashima
SB＝博報堂　HAKUHODO INC.

交通広告
Transport Advertisement

34

e リアルな〝つらら〟を溶かすことで
あたたかさを伝える
カップスープの車内広告

スープのあたたかさを印象深く伝えるため、
電車内に〝つらら〟を再現。光の反射や溶けかけの様子を
綿密に考慮しながらプラスチックを精密に型抜きし、
雪のようなスプレーを噴霧するなどリアルさを徹底した。

A cup soup advertisement that
conveys an impression of warmth by
melting realistic "icicles"

"Icicles" were recreated inside trains to strikingly convey an
impression of the warmth of the soup. Plastic was carefully molded
and the "icicles" coated with snow-like spray in an effort to make
them look as real as possible, with particular attention paid to
capturing the reflective qualities and melting effect of real icicles.

OUT-DOOR ADVERTISEMENT
屋外広告

TRANSPORT ADVERTISEMENT
交通広告

IN-DOOR ADVERT SEMENT
屋内広告

adidas 2003 Football 〝Own the game〟キャンペーン
adidas 2003 Football "Own the game" Campaign

スポーツブランド Sport Brand ｜ Japan

CL＝アディダスジャパン adidas Japan K.K.
CD＝ジョン万次郎 John Merrifield
AD＝クレメンタイン・トウレス Clementine Tourres
AD＝中島寛文 Hirofumi Nakajima
Production＝大谷昭徳（メディアコンシェルジュ）Akinori Otani (Media Concierge Inc.)
SB＝ティービーダブルエー・ジャパン（ワンエイティ・ティービーダブルエー）TBWA/JAPAN (180/TBWA)

屋外広告　Out-door Advertisement

ブランドメッセージを伝える
表現の限界にチャレンジした
屋外広告

10階建てのビルの高さにあるビルボードに
2人のサッカー選手が吊られ垂直のピッチでサッカーをプレイ。
アスリートたちと共有する、限界を超えたいという
ブランドメッセージを今までにないかたちで伝えた。

Outdoor advertising that takes communicating a brand message to the absolute limits

Two soccer players are suspended on a billboard as high as
a 10-storied building and play soccer on a vertical pitch.
In a way never seen before, the billboard communicated the
message that the brand shared the same desire of the athletes to
surpass limits.

11

Mondo Pasta 〝ロープパスタ〟キャンペーン
Mondo Pasta "Nudelschlürler" Campaign

食料品メーカー Foodstuff Manufacturer │ Germany

CL＝Mondo Pasta Gesskenberger & Arena
CD＝Doerle Spengler-Ahrens
CD＝Jan Rexhausen
AD＝Pablo Schencke
P＝Uwe Huettner, Fotostudio Huettner/Partners
CW＝Sergio Penzo
SB＝Jung von Matt

屋外広告 Out-door Advertisement

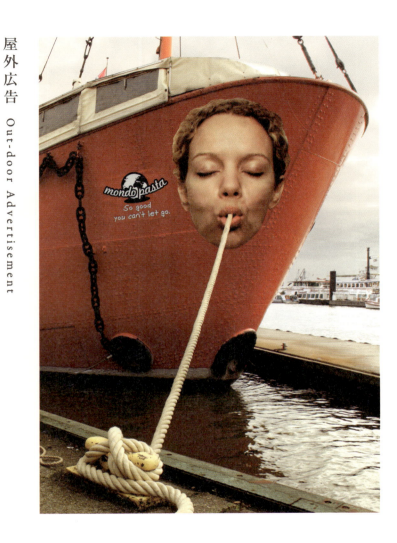

船を係留するロープを パスタに見立て 販売促進をねらった屋外広告

少ない予算で結果を出すため型破りな方法をとった。
プロモーションの場所に人が集まる港を選択し、
船の側面にパスタをすすっている顔の巨大なポスターを貼り、
ロープをパスタに見立てた。

An outdoor sales promotion advertisement that likens pasta to a rope mooring a boat

An unconventional method was used to achieve results
with a limited budget.
A popular harbor was chosen as the site for the promotion,
and posters with a large face sucking in pasta were pasted
on the sides of the boats, with the moorings likened to pasta.

〝紙の煉瓦壁、紙の鉄壁、紙の壁画、紙の魚用水槽〟キャンペーン
Paper Brick Wall, Paper Steel Wall, Paper Mural, Paper Fish Tank Campaign

印刷 Printing │ Malaysia

CL＝Hewlett-packard Malaysia
CD＝Andy Soong
CD＝Lisa Ng
AD＝Lee Foong Peng
AD＝Loo Kok Seng
P＝Jesse Choo (UNTOLD IMAGES)
CW＝Teh Le Vin
SB＝Publicis, Malaysia

屋外広告　Out-door Advertisement

通行人の目をだます 高品質の写真用紙の 屋外広告

紙が折れたようになっている写真用紙で作成された屋外広告。
壁の一角に貼ることによって、実物の壁が写真用紙を使用した
ポスターのように見える仕組み。

An outdoor advertisement for high-quality photographic paper that tested the eyesight of passersby

One corner of this poster made using photographic paper appears to be folded over like a sheet of paper. Several posters were pasted up around town, and the fact that the folded corner appeared real to the eyes of passersby actually proved that the poster was a reproduction made using high-quality photographic paper.

CL=ユニリーバ・ジャパン Unilever JapanK.K.
CD+CW=横澤宏一郎 Koichiro Yokozawa
AD+D=倉田潤一 Junichi Kurata
D=鈴木 学 Manabu Suzuki
P=高橋秀行 Hideyuki Takahashi
SB=博報堂 HAKUHODO INC.

屋外広告 Out-door Advertisement

マイクロカプセルを
〝プチプチ〟になぞらえた
シャンプーの立体ポスター

髪の潤いを守るマイクロカプセル配合のシャンプーの広告。
目に見えないマイクロカプセルを緩衝材の〝プチプチ〟により
視覚化。チープにならないよう、手作りで大きさ、色など
様々なパターンを検証し丁寧に制作した。

A three dimensional poster for shampoo that uses "bubbles" to simulate microcapsules

An advertisement for shampoo containing microcapsules that protect the hair's moistness. The invisible microcapsules are represented by the "bubbles" found in cushioning material. The poster was carefully designed and various combinations of sizes and colors actually verified to ensure the end result didn't look cheap.

14

AXEの新製品バイスのキャンペーン用OOH
OOH Advertising Campaign for the new AXE body fragrance Vice

化粧品メーカー Cosmetic Manufacturer ｜ Japan

CL＝ユニリーバ・ジャパン Unilever Japan K.K.
D＝山田誠也 Seiya Yamada
CW＝川村真司 Masashi Kawamura
P＝半田也寸志 Yasushi Handa
ACD＝辻本忠 Tadashi Tsujimoto
ECD＝スティーブ・エルリック Steve Elrick
SB＝ビービーエイチ トウキョウ BBH TOKYO

屋外広告 Out-door Advertisement

15

時間ごとに女性の下着が
透けて見える男性用
フレグランスの巨大看板

巨大ボードに綿ポリ素材で製作したブラウスをミシンで縫い付け、
1時間ごとに降水機から水を流すとブラジャーが透け
30分程で乾いて元に戻る仕掛け。
TVCMの音楽とナレーションを降水の始まりと連動して流した。

A giant billboard advertising a men's fragrance
on which female underwear is visible
at regular intervals during the day

A gimmick that involved sewing a blouse made of polyester-cotton fabric
onto a giant billboard and pouring water over it every hour so that the blouse became
see-through revealing a bra underneath. The blouse dried and the scene returned to
normal after 30 minutes. TVCM music and announcements were broadcast to
coincide with the start of each 'downpour'.

おデブファミリー キャンペーン
Overweight Family Campaign

食料品メーカー Foodstuff Manufacturer │ Japan

CL=味の素　AJINOMOTO CO., INC.
CD+AD=谷一和志　Kazushi Taniichi
D=小塚泰彦　Yasuhiko Kozuka
D=岡田佳子　Keiko Okada
CW=小林孝悦　Takayoshi Kobayashi
P=宇佐美雅浩　Masahiro Usami
DF=オーパーツ　OOPARTS
SB=博報堂　HAKUHODO INC.

屋外広告　Out-door Advertisement

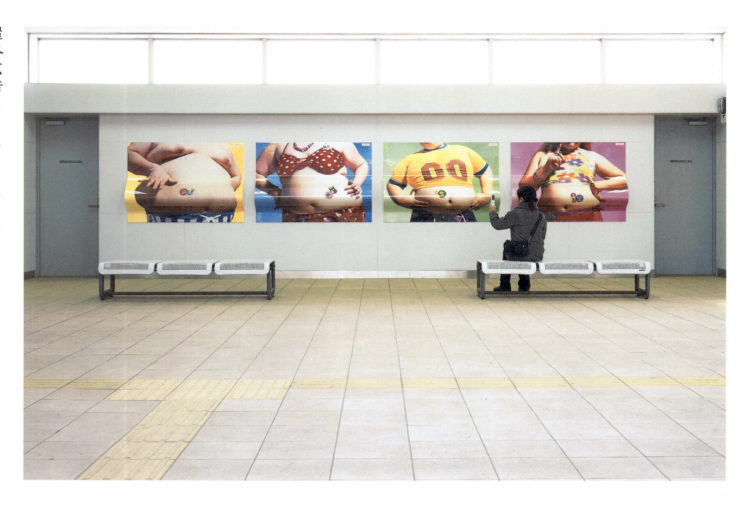

ポスターを弛ませ
〝たぷたぷお腹〟を表現した
カロリーオフ商品のポスター

ポスターを弛ませて〝たぷたぷに太ったお腹〟のように見せ、
食による健康をメッセージ。〝張り〟を表現できる強い紙を選び、
より情けない印象を強めるために、
〝能天気〟な衣装とライティング、撮影を心がけた。

A poster for a range of low-calorie products that represents a bulging stomach by "loosening" the poster

The poster is pasted "loosely" to make it look like a bulging stomach, sending a message about the health benefits of a change in diet. Strong paper able to express "firmness" was chosen and an effort made to use "laid-back" clothing, lighting and photography to create an even more woeful impression.

I.C.U. ガラス窓クリーナー キャンペーン
I.C.U. Glass and Window Cleaner Campaign

日用品メーカー Household Product Manufacturer ｜ South Africa

CL＝Adcock Ingram
CD＝Theo Ferreira
AD＝Nadja Lossgott
P＝David Prior
Writer＝Stuart Turner
Retouching＝Rob Frew
SB＝TBWA \ HUNT \ LASCARIS

17

等身大の人間ステッカーを使用した ガラス用クリーナーの広告

さまざまな場所のガラスのドアや窓に、
ガラスにぶつかる等身大の人間のステッカーを貼ることで、
そこにあることに気づかないぐらいガラスがきれいになる
製品の洗浄効果を宣伝した。

An advertisement for glass cleaner that uses a life-size sticker of a person

Touts the cleaning ability of the product, which renders
glass so clean that people fail to notice it's even there,
by attaching a life-size sticker of a person bumping
into the glass to doors and windows in various locations.

ミニクーパー〝Size〟キャンペーン
MINI COOPER Size Campaign

自動車メーカー Automobile Manufacturer │ Switzerland

CL＝BMW / MINI
CD＝Michael Rottmann
CD＝Alexander Jaggy
AD＝David Hanselmann
AD＝Hendrik Schweder
D＝Alban Schelbert
CW＝Lars Haensell
CW＝Ole Kleinhans
SB＝Jung von Matt, Zurich

18

ミニ・クーパーの車内は
おどろくほど広いことを示す
だまし絵ポスター

実物大のミニクーパーに大勢の人が乗り込み、
また降りていくだまし絵（トロンプルイユ）を利用したポスター。
地下鉄の地上出入口に貼られ、狭いと思われている
ミニクーパーの乗り心地が、実際には大きな車と
変わらないことを表現した。

A trompe l'oeil poster designed
to show just how roomy the
interior of the Mini Cooper

A poster that employs the technique of trompe l'oeil to show a
crowd of people getting in and out of a full-size Mini Cooper.
Designed to show that the Mini Cooper, which people think
is cramped inside, is actually just as comfortable to ride in as a big car.

健康で強い歯をユーモラスに表現した
ペットフードの屋外広告

屋外の遮断機に切り抜きボードの実物大の犬が噛み付いている。
ゲートが上に開いても犬は噛み付いたままで、
健康的なペットフードを与えれば犬の歯がどんなに丈夫になるかを
ユーモラスに大げさに表現した。

An outdoor advertisement for pet food
that expressed the idea of healthy, strong
teeth in a humorous fashion

A life-size cutout of a dog has its teeth fastened into an outdoor
crossing arm. The dog remains stuck to the gate even when it goes up,
expressing in a humorous and over the top way just how strong a dog's
teeth will get if it's fed healthy pet food.

CL＝IAMS
CD＝David Nobay
AD＝Eron Broughton
D＝Steve May
SB＝Saatchi＋Saatchi

屋外広告 Out-door Advertisement

19

春花のブーケ キャンペーン
Spring Blossoms Bouquet Campaign

花屋 Flower Shop｜India

CL＝Spring Blossoms
CD＋AD＋D＝Ashok Lad
CD＝Agnello Dias
CD＝Mahendra Bhagat
CD＋CW＝Amitabh Agnihotri
P＝Umesh Ahire
P＝Vishwanath Naik
DF＋SB＝JWT, India

屋外広告 Out-door Advertisement

20

花咲く街路樹をブーケに見立てた
フラワーショップの屋外広告

花の咲いた木を花束へと変身させ、花の新鮮さを
言葉で伝えるのではなく、〝見せる〟ことにした。
すべての花束の下には金属のフレームがあり、
実際の花束用のラッピングペーパーとサテンを使用した。

An outdoor advertisement for a flower
shop that likens flowering roadside trees
to bouquets

Flowering trees are transformed into bunches of flowers to convey an
impression of the freshness of flowers "visually" rather than in words.
All the bunches are supported by metal frames and wrapped in the same
wrapping paper and satin as actual bouquets.

ペプシライト〝細身の少女〟キャンペーン
Pepsi Light Skinny girl Campaign

飲料品メーカー Beverage Manufacturer │ Singapore

CL＝Pepsi
CD＝Francis Wee
AD＝Maurice Wee
AD＝Renee Lim
P＝Teo Studio
Retouching＝Procolor
DF＝BBDO, Singapore
SB＝Maurice Wee

屋外広告 Out-door Advertisement

21

ばかばかしいほど 細さを強調した 低カロリー清涼飲料水の広告

体型を気にする人向けに最適な飲み物だと伝えるため、
美容業界の細さへの執着をヒントに、モデルがどれほど
ばかばかしく細いか強調。スリムにしたことで、雑誌の背や
笑ってしまうほど狭い場所で広告が展開できた。

An advertisement for a low-calorie soft drink that emphasizes thinness to an almost ridiculous extent

In order to communicate that this drink is ideal for people concerned about their figure, the advertisement takes a hint from the fashion industry's obsession with thinness and emphasizes how ridiculously thin the models are. Due to their thinness the advertisements could be placed on the spines of magazines and other almost laughably narrow spaces.

ルノー〝オープンカー〟広告看板 キャンペーン
Renault Convetible Billboard Campaign

自動車メーカー Automobile Manufacturer │ Switzerland

CL＝Reuault
CD＝Philipp Skrabal
AD＝Daniel Kobi
D＝Isabelle Hanses
SB＝Publicis, Zurich

屋外広告 Out-door Advertisement

看板から飛び出した車でオープンカーを運転する喜びを伝える広告

自動車購入の可能性がある人に、このオープンカーに乗ると、彼らがどれほど太陽に近いかを3次元で経験させるという着想より制作。特注のアルミ部品を作成し、常識の枠を超えたデザインで看板に取り付けた。

Renault convertibleAn advertisement for a convertible that conveys the joy of driving in a way that's visually astounding

Created based on the concept of enabling people thinking about buying a car to experience in 3D the feeling of proximity to the sun one gets when riding in this convertible. Special aluminum components were custom made and attached to the billboard based on a design that exceeds the bounds of conventional wisdom.

オクトパスガーデン〝減速バンプ〟キャンペーン
Octopus Garden Speedbumps Campaign

ヘルスコンサルティング Health and Well-being │ Canada

CL＝Octopus Garden Yoga Studio
CD＝Stephen Jurisic
CD＝Angus Tucker
AD＝Nellie Kim
CW＝Chris Hirsch
SB＝john st. advertising

ビジネス街の歩道に設置した減速バンプで〝ゆとり〟を奨めるヨガ教室の広告

人々の注意を惹くには多少押し付けがましいものが必要と考え、あわただしいビジネス街の歩道に実際の減速バンプを設置し、ヨガ教室の助けを借りて〝スロウ・ダウン（ゆとりを持つ）〟ことを推奨した。

An advertisement for a yoga school that advocates "slowing down" by setting up a speed bump on the sidewalk in a business district

Mindful of the need to come up with something slightly obtrusive in order to attract people's attention, the designers hit upon the idea of conveying the message that people should consider "slowing down" with the help of the yoga school concerned by setting up an actual speed bump on the sidewalk in a busy business district.

LEGO 〝遊ぼう〟キャンペーン
LEGO Play on Campaign

玩具メーカー Toy Manufacturer｜Chili

CL＝LEGO
CD＝Cesar Agost Carreño
AD＝Sergio Iacobelli
AD＝Sebastian Alvarado
I＝Ricardo Salamanca
CW＝Felipe Mañalich
P＝Sotelo
SB＝Ogilvy & Mather, Chile

ビルがブロックでできているかのような
錯覚を引き起こす玩具ポスター

〝子どものように世界を見る〟をコンセプトに制作されたレゴのポスター。
実際のビルの壁面に戦略的にポスターを設置し、
あたかもビルがレゴブロックで建てられているかのように見せた。

A poster for a toy that creates an illusion in
which buildings appear to be made out of blocks

A poster for Lego created based on the concept of "looking at the world like a
child." The poster was placed strategically on the walls of actual buildings in such a
way that it looked as if the buildings were made out of Lego blocks.

〝ヒーー！ アーー！ アーッグ！〟キャンペーン
Heeeaa! Aaahhh! Aaargh! Campaign

テコンドー教室 Tae Kwon do School │ Singapore

CL＝JH KIM TAEKWANDO
CD＝Neil Johnson
CD＝Terrence Tan
AD＝Khalid Osman
CW＝Priti Kapur
P＝Allan Ng
SB＝Jolene Quek

屋外広告　Out-door Advertisement

テコンドーの破壊力を示す戦略的に貼られたポスター

テコンドー選手が破壊したかのように見える場所に
戦略的にポスターを設置し、テコンドーの強さを表現。
近くでテコンドー教室が開催されていることを
費用効率よく印象的に知らせた。

Posters placed strategically to emphasize the destructive power of tae kwon do

The power of tae kwon do was emphasized by strategically
placing posters on sites that looked as though they might have
been destroyed by a tae kwon do athlete. This informed people
in a way that was cost effective and striking that there was a tae
kwon do school in their area.

Kingfisher 〝ドアハンドル〟キャンペーン
Kingfisher Door Handle Campaign

飲料品メーカー Beverage Manufacturer │ India

CL＝UB Group
CD＝Agnello Dias
CD＝Mahendra Bhagat
CD＋AD＋D＝Ashok Lad
CD＋CW＝Amitabh Agnihotri
P＝Ashay Kshirsagar
P＝Sachin Powle
DF＋SB＝JWT, India

FedEx T シャツ
FedEx T-Shirt

配送サービス　Courier Service ｜ U.S.A

CL＝FedEx
CD＝David Lubars
ECD＝Eric Silver
AD＝Chuck Tso
CW＝Eric Schutte
DF＋SB＝BBDO, New York

いつでも荷物の配達中に見える
宅配便の封筒がプリントされたTシャツ

宅配便といえばいつでもどこでも FedEx であるということを表現。
本物の封筒をスキャンし、Tシャツの側面にシルクスクリーンでプリント。
低予算で作成できるため、各地で配布できるよう何千枚も印刷した。

A T-shirt featuring an envelope used by a courier service that's often seen making deliveries

Conveys the message that FedEx is a courier service that's seen all the time almost everywhere. An actual envelope was scanned and silkscreen printed on the front of the T-shirt. Because the T-shirt could be produced cheaply, thousands were printed and distributed everywhere.

屋外広告　Out-door Advertisement

バーの入り口の取っ手に設置する
ビアマグ型のステッカー広告

バーを訪れる客に商品を強く意識させるビアマグ型ステッカー広告。
インドではマスメディアでアルコール飲料の広告ができないため、
ドアを開けるたびに商品を意識するようバーの入り口で広告を展開した。

A sticker advertisement in the shape of a beer mug attached to a door handle at the entrance to a bar

A sticker advertisement in the shape of a beer mug designed to make patrons visiting the bar strongly aware of the product.
Because alcoholic drinks can't be advertised in the mass media in India, the advertisement was placed at the entrance to bars to make patrons aware of the product each time they open the door.

〝間違った労働環境〟キャンペーン
Wrong Working Environment Campaign

求人支援サービス Recruitment Service ｜ Germany

CL＝Jobsintown.de
CD＝Matthias Spaetgens
CD＝Jan Leube
CD＝Oliver Handlos
AD＝David Fischer
CW＝Daniel Bödeker
CW＝Alex Tischer
P＝Hans Starck

Styling＝Petra Hoefer
Styling＝Jessica Klimach
Styling＝CISEL
Account Supervisor＝Katrin Seegers
Account Supervisor＝Katrin Ploska
Account Supervisor＝Jana Wolotschij
SB＝Scholz & Friends Berlin

屋外広告　Out-door Advertisement

現在の仕事に満足していない人に向けた
転職・求人サイトのキャンペーン

コインランドリーや自動販売機の機械をインタラクティブに利用。
ぞっとするような状況下で働く人々をポスターでユーモラスに表現。
〝これはまさに自分が感じていることだ〟というリアクションを
引き出し、印象に残るようにした。

A job-transfer and recruitment website campaign
aimed at people dissatisfied with their existing jobs

Vending machines, a laundromat, and other pieces of machinery were used interactively
to portray in a humorous way people working in horrific conditions. The aim was to leave
an impression in people's minds by making them think, "This is exactly how I feel."

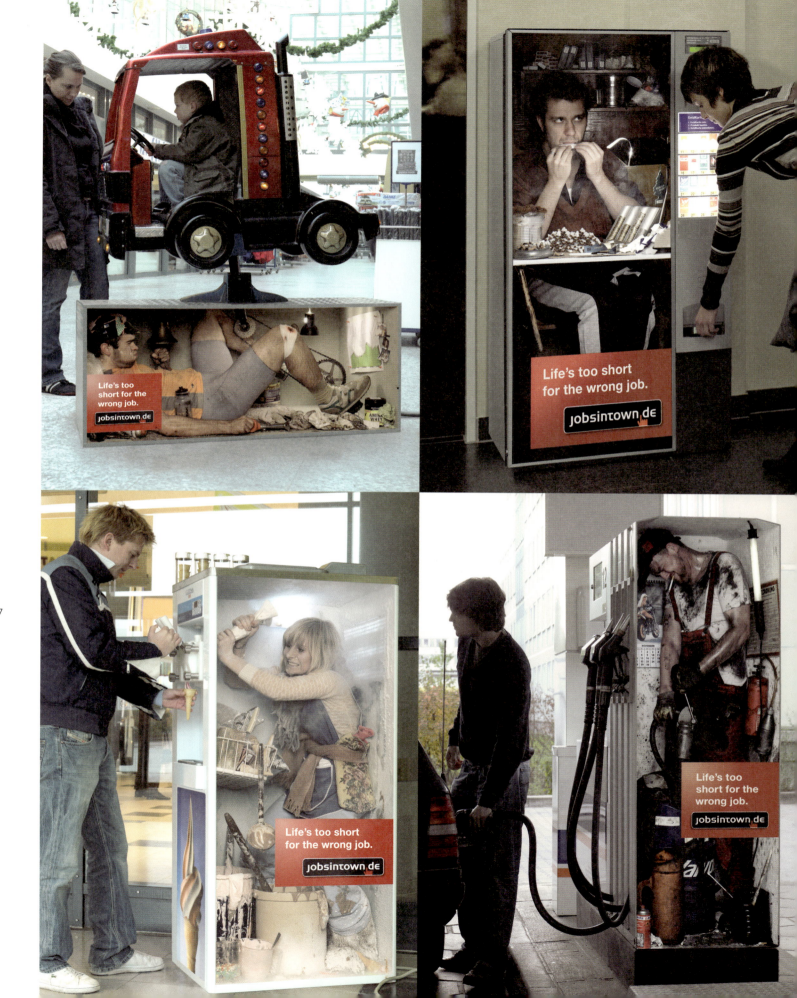

A Fitting Advertisement キャンペーン
A Fitting Advertisement Campaign

アパレル Apparel | Japan

CL=ワールド World Co., Ltd.
CD=永井一史 Kazufumi Nagai
CD=安藤宏治 Koji Ando
AD+D=細川 剛 Go Hosokawa
CW=渡辺潤平 Junpei Watanabe
P=青野千紘 Chihiro Aono

DF=博報堂 HAKUHODO INC.
Producer=角谷 悟 Satoru Kakutani
Producer=細谷まどか Madoka Hosoya
Producer=山室貞哲 Sadaaki Yamamuro
SB=博報堂 HAKUHODO INC.

服の良さを伝える
パブリックスペースでの
擬似試着キャンペーン

パブリックな場で服の良さが一番伝わる試着ができるよう、
幅12mの広告スペースに鏡を設置し、その鏡面にブランドの
洋服、バッグ、靴などの写真出力を貼り付けた。
鏡の前に立つと、擬似試着が体験できる。

A simulated fitting room in public designed to highlight the quality of a clothing line

A mirror was set up in a 12-meter-wide advertising space so
that people could 'try on' clothes, which is the best way to
emphasize their quality, in public. Photographs of clothes,
bags, shoes, and other items of the brand were stuck to the
mirror. By standing in front of the mirror, people could
experience what it would be like to try on the items.

ラフォーレ原宿グランドバザール告知広告
Laforet HARAJUKU Grand Bazar Announcement Advertisement

商業施設 Commercial Facility │ Japan

CL=ラフォーレ原宿 LAFORET HARAJUKU Co., Ltd.
CD＋AD=佐野研二郎 Kenjiro Sano
D=岡本和樹 Kazuki Okamoto
D=長嶋りかこ Rikako Nagashima
D=鈴木亜希子 Akiko Suzuki
P=山本光男 MItsuo Yamamoto
Film Director=田中秀幸 Hideyuki Tanaka
Film Director=保坂暁 Akira Hosoka
SB=MR_DESIGN

屋外広告 Out-door Advertisement

29

夜空に打ち上げられた花火を
Ｔシャツ6000枚で表現した告知広告

流行発信地であるラフォーレ原宿の夏のグランドバザール告知用屋外広告。
Ｔシャツや靴などのファッションアイテムを花火に見立てた。
実際にＴシャツ6000枚を並べて、高さ22mのクレーンで上に上がり撮影した。

A sale notification tool that likens T-shirts
to fireworks being launched into the sky

A sale notification tool for the summer grand bazaar at Laforet Harajuku, a major
starting point for fashion in Tokyo. T-shirts, shoes, and other fashion items are
likened to skyrockets. The photography involved lining up 6000 actual t-shirts
and hoisting them into the air using a 22-meter-high crane.

カッシーナ・イクスシー・プライベート オープン告知広告
Cassina ixc. PRIVATE Opening Announcement Advertisement

アパレル Apparel | Japan

CL=カッシーナ・イクスシー Cassina ixc. ltd.
CD+AD=石井 原 Gen Ishii
CD+CW=斉藤賢司 Kenji Saito
D=榮 良太 Ryota Sakae
D=山口範久 Norihisa Yamaguchi
P=森本徹也 Tetsuya Morimoto
DF=ツーブラトン two platon
SB=博報堂 HAKUHODO INC.

屋外広告 Out-door Advertisement

30

カーテンを使用し期待感を煽る家具ブランドの新ショップオープン告知

家具ブランドの新ショップオープン告知ポスター。本物のカーテンをポスターに付け、オープン当日にカーテンを開いた。ショップのコンセプト〝極私的空間〟を伝え、見る人の注目を促し期待感を煽ることに成功した。

Notification of the opening of a new furniture store that uses a curtain to conjure up a feeling of anticipation

A poster advertising the opening of a new furniture store. An actual curtain was draped over the poster and opened on the day the store opened. The poster successfully conveyed the store concept of "a strictly private space" and conjured up a feeling of anticipation by capturing the attention of viewers.

CL=日本放送出版協会 JAPAN BROADCAST PUBLISHING CO., LTD.
CD+CW=館 隆裕 Takahiro Tate
AD+D=西田 太 Futoshi Nishida
D=手島 瞳 Hitomi Tejima
CW=山本絵里子 Eriko Yamamoto
P=大西 剛 Go Onishi
I=大塚いちお Ichio Otsuka
DF=クリエイティブ オリコム Creative ORICOM CO., LTD.
SB=オリコム ORICOM CO., LTD.

楽しい気分になってもらうことを最優先に考えた料理雑誌のトレインジャック

強制的なコピーは一切排除し、楽しい気分になってもらうことを第一の目的とした。中吊りをアイ・キャッチに、その後、接した人が自発的に窓上のポスターを見たくなるような空間設計にした。

A train car domination for a cooking magazine in which top priority was given to putting commuters in a cheerful mood

All traces of insistent copy were removed and top priority given to putting commuters in a cheerful mood. Hanging advertisements were used primarily as attention getters, with the space designed so that people who viewed them naturally felt the urge to look at the posters above the windows.

黒烏龍茶のモビール型中吊りキャンペーン
A mobile-style in-train Advertising Campaign for black oolong tea

飲料品メーカー Beverage Manufacturer | Japan

CL=サントリー SUNTORY LIMITED.
CD=澤本嘉光 Yoshimitsu Sawamoto
AD=えぐちりか Rika Eguchi
D=渡辺亮 Ryo Watanabe
CW=倉成英俊 Hidetoshi Kuranari
P=青山たかかず Takakazu Aoyama
DF=JCスパーク J. C. SPARK
Art=半澤強 Tsuyoshi Hanzawa
Producer=杉本哲也 Tetsuya Sugimoto
SB=電通 DENTSU Inc.

交通広告 Transport Advertisement

32

油っこい食事の食品サンプルを利用したモビールのような中吊り広告

焼肉、揚げ物、天ぷらなど合計6種類の油っこい食事の
食品サンプルそのものを、モビールのようにつるして
黒烏龍茶でバランスをとった中吊り広告。
黒烏龍茶があれば食のバランスがとれることを表現した。

Mobile-like hanging advertisements using display models of greasy foods

Hanging advertisements in the form of mobiles that used actual display models of greasy foods such as yakiniku, deep-fried foods, and tempura balanced with black oolong tea. The ads promoted the idea that drinking black oolong tea enables one to maintain a balanced diet.

〝クノールカップスープ〟つらら中吊り広告
"Knoll Cup Soup" Icicle Hunging Advertisement

飲食料品メーカー Foodstuff Manufacturer │ Japan

CL=味の素 AJINOMOTO CO., INC.
CD+AD=谷一和志 Kazushi Taniichi
D=小塚泰彦 Yasuhiko Kozuka
D=中島淳志 Atsushi Nakajima
CW=小林孝悦 Takayoshi Kobayashi
P=大手仁志 Hitoshi Ote
CG=中島輝子 Teruko Nakashima
SB=博報堂 HAKUHODO INC.

交通広告
Transport Advertisement

リアルな〝つらら〟を溶かすことで あたたかさを伝える カップスープの車内広告

スープのあたたかさを印象深く伝えるため、
電車内に〝つらら〟を再現。光の反射や溶けかけの様子を
綿密に考慮しながらプラスチックを精密に型抜きし、
雪のようなスプレーを噴霧するなどリアルさを徹底した。

A cup soup advertisement that conveys an impression of warmth by melting realistic "icicles"

"Icicles" were recreated inside trains to strikingly convey an impression of the warmth of the soup. Plastic was carefully molded and the "icicles" coated with snow-like spray in an effort to make them look as real as possible, with particular attention paid to capturing the reflective qualities and melting effect of real icicles.

〝ドラゴンボール〟DVD 発売告知キャンペーン
"Dragon Ball" DVD Sales Announcement Campaign

出版／テレビ局／映画配給 Publishing / Broadcast / Film Production, Distribution ｜ Japan

CL＝集英社、フジテレビ、東映 SHUEISHA Inc., Fuji Television, TOEI COMPANY, INC.
CD＝長谷部守彦 Morihiko Hasebe
AD＋D＝倉田潤一 Junichi Kurata
D＝齋藤浩正（バッファローディー）Kosei Saito (baffalo-D)
CW＝坂本仁 Hitoshi Sakamoto
CW＝宇野元基 Motoki Uno
DF＝バッファローディー baffalo-D
SB＝博報堂 HAKUHODO INC.

交通広告
Transport Advertisement

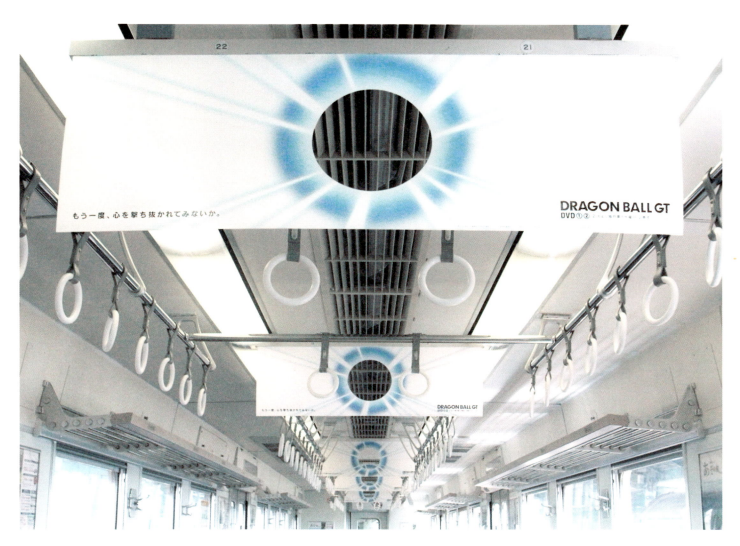

広告自体をコンテンツ化して、見る人に楽しんでもらうアニメ DVD 発売告知

電車内の左端と右端の中吊りに、主人公の必殺技のかめはめ波を出す手の
ビジュアルを配置。その間の中吊りすべてに穴を開けて中吊りが打ち抜かれたように
見える仕掛けをつくり、車内にかめはめ波を出現させた。

An advertisement notifying people about the release of an anime DVD that aims to delight viewers by turning the advertisement itself into contents

Kamehameha were made to appear in trains using a gimmick that involved arranging visuals of the Kamehameha energy blast employed by several characters in the DVD in the left- and right-hand hanging advertisements and actually creating holes in the hanging advertisements in between so that it liked like they'd been punched through by the blast.

ルノー 〝バスいっぱいの枕〟キャンペーン
Renault Pillows on Bus Campaign

自動車メーカー Automobile Manufacturer｜Switzerland

CL＝Renault
CD＝Philipp Skrabal
AD＝Daniel Kobi
D＝Isabelle Hanses
SB＝Publicis, Zurich

安全性を演出した
モーターショー来訪者向けの
交通広告

ルノーの工場はヨーロッパ一安全な自動車の生産ラインであり、
どれほどルノーの自動車が安全で、衝撃から保護してくれるのかを
枕を使用して演出。巨大なデジタル出力で、
車の輪郭にそってジュネーブの公共交通バスを包み込んだ。

A transport advertisement
aimed at motor show visitors
that focuses on safety

Renault's factories produce the safest automobiles in Europe,
and this advertisement stresses how safe Renault automobiles
are and the extent to which they protect the occupants in the
event of a collision. The advertisements took the form of
giant digital printouts that were wrapped around public buses
in Geneva in such a way that they followed the contours of
the bus.

スキーキャビン キャンペーン
Ski Cabin Campaign

レジャー Leisure｜Netherlands

CL＝Centerparcs Europe
CD＋AD＝Darre van Dijk
CD＝Piebe Piebenga
AD＝Martun de Jong
P＋I＝Arno Bosma
SB＝Ogilvy Amsterdam

電車の車体がスキー場とゴンドラに
変身したリゾートパークのキャンペーン

ヨーロッパ各地でリゾートパークを運営する企業の
広告キャンペーンの一環。路面電車の白い車体に、
パンタグラフ部分をフックに見立てスキー場のゴンドラを描いた。

A campaign for a resort park in which
the exterior of a streetcar was transformed
into a ski field and gondola

Part of a campaign for a company that runs resort parks all over
Europe. A ski area gondola was painted onto the white exterior of a
streetcar, with the pantograph made to look like the gondola hook.

シャークバス キャンペーン
SHARK Bus Campaign

出版 Publishing │ Netherlands

CL＝National Geographic Channel
CD＋AD＝Darre van Dijk
CD＝Piebe Piebenga
P＋I＝Fulco Smit Roeters
SB＝Amsterdam Advertising

交通広告 Transport Advertisement

バスの乗降口を
ホオジロザメの口に
見立てたラッピングバス

肉食動物のドキュメンタリー番組を宣伝する
ラッピングバス。バスの乗降口が巨大なホオジロザメの
口の部分になっており、乗客はするどい牙が
生えた口に飲み込まれていく。

A bus wrapping that involved making
the entrance to the bus look like the
mouth of a great white shark

A bus wrapping promoting a documentary program on
carnivorous animals. The entrance to the bus looks like the mouth
of a giant great white shark, with all the passengers being eaten
up in the mouth with its razor-sharp teeth.

ペプシライト トラック キャンペーン
Pepsi light truck Campaign

飲料品メーカー Beverage Manufacturer │ Germany

CL＝Pepsico Deutschland GMBH
CD＝Sebastian Hardieck
CD＝Raphael Milczarer
AD＝Fabian Kirner
AD＝Yoerg Sachtleben
P＝Simone Rosenberg
P＝Svensou Linnert
CW＝Felix Lemcqe
SB＝BBDO Duesseldolf GMBH

どれほど低カロリーであるかを
宙で浮いたペプシライトの
ポスターで表現した広告

ターゲット層がまさに購入を検討する〝路上〟でインパクトを
与えるため、実際のトラックの荷台側面から積荷が
透けて見えているかのように表現。
積荷は宙に浮いており製品がいかに低カロリーであるかを伝えた。

An advertisement for a soft
drink that uses the side of a
large transport truck

In order to have an impact 'on the street' where the target demographic
is likely to consider buying the product, the advertisement was designed
so that it looked like a load of the actual product could be seen through
the side of a truck. The load appears to be floating in the air, drawing
attention to the fact the product is a low-calorie soft drink.

OTTO 〝スパイホール〟キャンペーン
OTTO Spyhole Campaign

アパレル Apparel │ Germany

CL＝OTTO
CD＝Sven Klohk
CD＝Ulrich Zünkeler
AD＝Rolf Leger
CW＝Stefan Wübbe
Gaphic Designer＝Caroline Rathgeber
P＝Leif Schmodde
SB＝Kolle Rebbe Werbeagentur GmbH

水着姿の人気モデルが
玄関先に見えるゲリラ広告

玄関のぞき穴の外側に設置するオットーの通販カタログの広告。
配達人の呼び鈴を聞いてのぞき穴から玄関先を確認すると、
まるでスーパーモデルのエバ・パドバーグがカタログを届けに
玄関前にいるかのように見える。

Guerilla advertising that makes a
popular model appear at people's front
door in a swimsuit

An advertisement for the Otto mail order catalog that's placed on the
outside of the peephole in people's front door. When they look through
the peephole after hearing the delivery person ring the doorbell, they
sees what appears to be supermodel Eva Padberg delivering their catalog.

ユニリーバ〝AXE〟キャンペーン
Unilever − AXE Campaign

日用品、化粧品メーカー Commodity, Cosmetic Manufacturer ｜ UAE

CL＝Unilever - AXE
CD＋CW＝Clinton Manson
CD＋AD＝Dominic Stallard
CW＝Ma'n Abu Taleb
SB＝Lowa Mena / Dubai

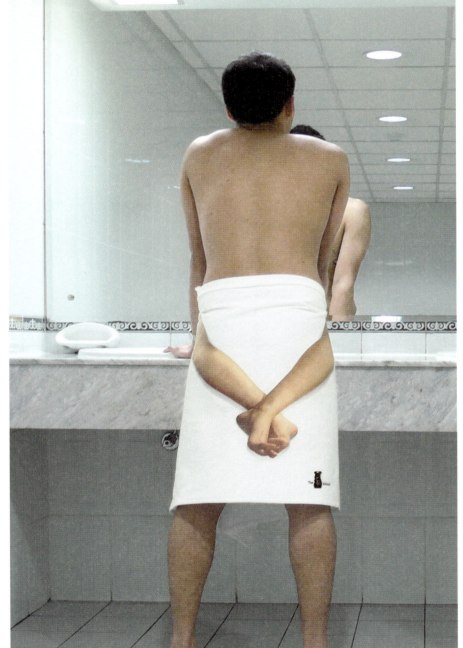

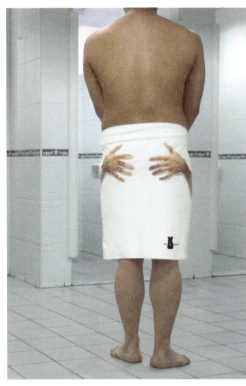

屋内広告 In-door Advertisement

製品使用の〝モテ〟効果を暗示する男性化粧品ブランドの広告

〝使えば女性にモテる〟を一貫して打ち出す男性化粧品ブランドAXE。小太りの男性が腰に巻いたバスタオルには、女性の腕や脚がプリントしてあり、製品使用の効果をショッキングかつユーモラスに暗示している。

An advertisement for a male cosmetics brand that hints at the effect the product has on women

AXE is a male cosmetics brand that consistently boasts that using its products will make men "popular with females." The advertisement hints at the effect using the product will have in a way that's shocking yet humorous by depicting a pudgy male with a bath towel wrapped around his waist on which are printed female arms and legs.

41

Wilson 〝破損テニスボール〟キャンペーン
Wilson crashing tennis ball Campaign

スポーツメーカー Sports Manufacturer │ Switzerland

CL＝Wilson Sporting Goods Co.
CD＝Philipp Sicrabal
AD＝Daniel Kobi
D＝Isabelle Hanser
SB＝Publicis, Zurich

ウィルソンのテニスラケットが
発揮する力強さを
劇的に表現したステッカー広告

このラケットでボールにコンタクトすると22パーセント増しの
力が出るという事実をもとに制作。本物のテニスボールを
半分に切って、まるでボールがめり込んでいるかのように
透明なプラスティックに接着した。

A tennis racquet advertisement that
dramatically evokes the power
unleashed by the actual product

Created based on the fact that using this racquet results in a
22% increase in power when contact is made with the ball. A
real tennis ball was cut in half and glued to clear plastic so
that it looks as though the ball has caved in.

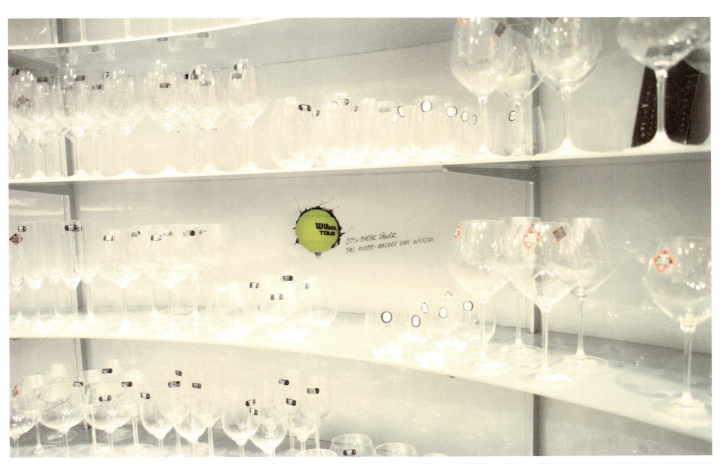

43

The School of Visual Arts 〝THINK 考える〟キャンペーン
The School of Visual Arts "THINK" Campaign

学校 School｜U.S.A

CL＝The School of Visual Arts
CD＋AD＋SB＝Frank Anselmo
AD＝Jeseok Yi
P＝Billy Siegrist
DF＝KNARF

屋内広告　In-door Advertisement

44

浮かんだ考えをどこでも書きとめられる
美術系大学のキャンペーン

スクール・オブ・ビジュアル・アーツでは創造的な思想家たちが
教鞭を取っている。このキャンペーンでは、そんな伝統を反映し、
あらゆるところで〝THINK 考える〟ことを奨励し、考えを書きとめる
場所を提供した。

A campaign for an art school that provides room
for people to write down all kinds of thoughts
regardless of where they occur

The School of Visual Arts is a place where creative thinkers are welcomed onto
the staff. Reflecting this tradition, this campaign encouraged thinking in all kinds
of locations by providing room for people to jot down their ideas.

'Hangers゛キャンペーン
Hangers Campaign

救世軍 Salvation Army │ Argentina

CL＝Salvation Army
CD＝Javier Mentasti
CD＝Christian Camean
CD＝Ramiro Crosio
AD＝Ezequiel Orlandi
CW＝Damian Issak
P＝Daniel Maestri
SB＝JWT, Argentina

屋内広告 In-door Advertisement

45

試着室に設置した救世軍からの服の寄付の呼びかけ立体広告

試着室の内部に、生活困窮者が施しを請うかのように
手を伸ばしているポスターを設置。その手の部分に
プラスチックの指を付け洋服フックとした。
新しい服を買うときに、不要になる衣服の寄付を意識させた。

An appeal for donations of clothes to the Salvation Army in fitting rooms

Posters of a needy person extending their hand as if
asking for help were displayed in fitting rooms. A hook
for clothes in the form of a plastic finger was attached to
the hand, prompting people to consider donating
clothes they no longer need when buying new clothes.

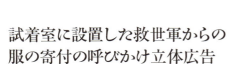

Jelly Tots Sweets 〝水中世界〟エレベーター キャンペーン
Jelly Tots Sweets "Underwater World" Elevator Campaign

菓子製造・販売 Confectionaries Manufacturer, Sales │ South Africa

CL=Tiger Brands
ECD=Damon Stapleton
CD=Bibi Lotter
AD=Kursten Meyer
AD=Chris Crawford
AD=Tammy Mattison
D+DF=N \ A
P=David Prior
I=Angus Cameron
SB=TBWA \ HUNT \ LASCARIS, Johannesburg

屋内広告 In-door Advertisement

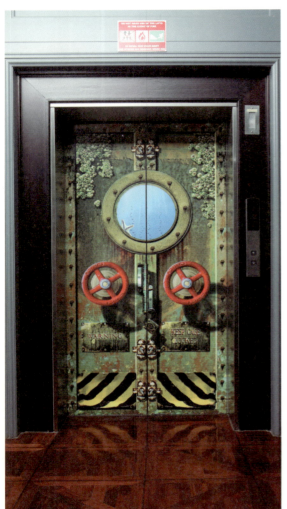

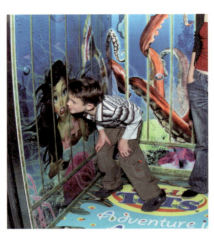

46

エレベーターの中で
水中世界の冒険ができる
子ども向けの菓子の広告

製品のブランド・ポジショニング〝どこでも冒険〟を
実現させるために、体験エレベーターを各地ショッピング
モールに設置。人魚や水中生物のリアルなイラストや
水中の音を使い、エレベーターを水中世界へと変えた。

A confectionery advertisement aimed at children that enables them to go on an adventure in an underwater world

In order to realize the product's brand positioning of "experiencing adventure anywhere," elevators offering a unique experience where installed in shopping centers around the country. Using realistic illustrations of mermaids and various forms of marine life as well as underwater sounds, the elevators were transformed into underwater worlds.

CL＋DF＝BBDO, New York
CD＋AD＋SB＝Frank Anselmo
CD＋AD＝Jayson Atienza
P＝Billy Siegrist
Chief Creative Officers＝David Lubars
Chief Creative Officers＝Bill Bruce

屋内広告　In-door Advertisement

PCモニターにクレヨンで 落書きしたかのような 社内イベント告知フィルム

〝子どもを会社に連れてこよう〟というイベントを子ども心を
体現する方法で社内に告知。クレヨンで落書きした透明な
アセレートフィルムを、夜遅くこっそりと社内すべての
500台以上のPCモニターに貼り付けた。

An internal notice for an event that looks as though someone has written on PC monitors in crayon

An event that involved bringing children along to the office was
advertised in a way that embodied childhood innocence.
Late at night, transparent acetate film that had been written on
in crayon was stuck surreptitiously to all of the more than 500
PC monitors in the office.

Milky Way 〝ベルト・コンベア〟キャンペーン
Milky Way "Conveyer Belt" Campaign

菓子製造 Confectionaries Manufacturer │ U.S.A

CL＝Milky Way
Executive Creative Director＝Greg Hahn
CD＋CW＝Scott Kaplan
CD＋CW＝Tom Kraemer
AD＋SB＝Frank Anselmo
AD＝Jayson Atienza
P＝Billy Siegrist
Chief Creative Officer＝David Lubars
Chief Creative Officer＝Bill Bruce
DF＝BBDO

レジのベルト・コンベアを利用した
キャラメル入りチョコバーの広告

おいしいキャラメルがたっぷり入っていることをレジの
ベルト・コンベアを利用して表現。半分は固定部分、
半分がベルト部分についており、ベルト・コンベアが動くと、
キャラメルがずっと伸びていくようになっている。

An advertisement for a caramel chocolate bar that uses a checkout belt conveyor

The fact that the bar was full of delicious caramel was
emphasized by using a checkout belt conveyor. Half of the
advertisement was attached to the stationary part, and half to
the moving part of the conveyor, so that when the conveyor
moved the "caramel" kept stretching.

Doguitos "モバイル" キャンペーン
Doguitos Mobile Campaign

ペット用品メーカー Pet Goods Manufacturer | Brazil

CL＝Nestlé Purina Petcare
CD＝Milton Mastrocessário
AD＝Alexandre Silveira
P＝Marcelo Ribeiro
I＝Marcos Cézar
SB＝Maccann Erickson Brazil

Your dog does crazy things for Doguitos.

49

犬の夢中さを伝える
ドッグフードの店内ディスプレイ

犬がこの製品を手にいれるためならなんでもすることを表現し、
どんなに犬がこの製品に夢中になるかを
犬の飼い主に伝えようとした。宣伝マテリアルの一つは
商品の店頭ディスプレイの真上に設置するよう作られた。

An in-store display for dog food that conveys the obsession of dogs

An attempt to convey to dog owners the degree to which dogs might become obsessed with the product by suggesting the lengths to which they might go to get their paws on it. One component of the publicity material was designed to be installed directly above in-store displays of the product concerned.

S.E.A〝強力な電池〟キャンペーン
S.E.A Powerful Battery Campaign

電機メーカー Electric Manfacturer ｜ Malaysia

CL＝Gillette Management (S.E.A)
CD＝Daniel Comar
CD＝Tham Khai Meng
CD＝Brenda Boler
AD＝James Wong
AD＝Gary Hor
AD＝Tham Khai Meng
P＝Wizard Photography
SB＝Ogilvy & Mather Advertising

Standard Bank 冷蔵庫マグネット
Standard Bank Fridge Magnet

銀行 Bank ｜ South Africa

CL＝Standard Bank (Achiever Account)
ECD＝Damon Stapleton
CD＋CW＝Nicholas Hulley
AD＝Nadja Lossgott
P＝David Prior
CW＝Stuart Turner
Stylist＝Michelle Wastie
SB＝TBWA \ HUNT \ LASCARIS

屋内広告 In-door Advertisement

50

エスカレーターを利用し強力な電池を表現した屋外広告

電池の強力さ、耐久性を表現するために、電池が蓋で半分隠れたシールを作成。エスカレーターを動かしているかのように見える仕掛け。大きなショッピングモールの通行量の多いエスカレーターに設置した。

An outdoor advertisement that used a moving sidewalk to express the idea of a powerful battery

In order to symbolize a battery's strength and endurance, a seal depicting a battery partly concealed by a cover was produced and attached to a busy moving sidewalk in a large shopping mall so that it looked like the battery was powering the moving sidewalk.

冷蔵庫を看板に見立てた銀行の学生向けキャンペーン

学生は銀行を嫌っており通常の広告では効果が薄い。学生の冷蔵庫とは真逆の高級品や珍味でいっぱいであるかのような目の錯覚を引き起こすだまし絵が印刷された冷蔵庫マグネットを配布し、効果的に浸透を狙った。

A bank campaign aimed at students in which a refrigerator is transformed into a sign

Students have an aversion to banks and so normal advertisements are largely ineffective. This advertisement aimed to get the message across effectively by distributing fridge magnets on which were printed trompe l'oeil pictures designed to deceive the eye into thinking the fridge was full of the kinds of luxury items and rare goods unlikely to be found in a student's fridge.

POSTER
ポスター

NEWSPAPER ADVERTISEMENT
新聞広告

CATALOG
カタログ

DIRECT MAIL
ダイレクトメール

BUSINESS CARD
名刺

Art Foco ブランディングポスター
Art Foco Branding Poster

眼鏡店 Optician's shop │ Brazil

CL＝Art Foco
CD＝Marcello Serpa
CD＝Lui'z Sanches
AD＋D＝Gustavo Victorino
CW＝Cesar Herszkowicz
P＝HUGOTREU
SB＝Almap BBDO / Sao Paulo

ポスター　Poster

女性がだんだんと服を脱いでいく眼鏡店の視力検査表風ポスター

世界的に使用されている視力検査表をベースに作成。
非常にユーモラスな方法で新規オープンの眼鏡店に注目させ、
友達の間で話題になるようにした。ポスターは店内に展示、
または顧客にプレゼントとして郵送された。

A poster for an optician's shop modeled on an eyesight test chart in which a woman gradually removes her clothes

Created based on the eyesight test chart used around the world.
Designed to focus attention in an extremely humorous way on a
newly opened optician's shop and become a topic of discussion
among friends. The poster was displayed inside the store and
mailed out to customers as a gift.

GOOD EYESIGHT IS FUNDAMENTAL

ArtFoco
Prescription Glasses

52

Flower Magic ブランディングポスター
Flower Magic Branding Poster

フラワーメーカー Flower Manufacturer │ Japan

CL=モンソーフルール　MONCEAU FLEURS
CD=斉藤太郎　Taro Saito
AD=戸田宏一郎　Koichiro Toda
CW=志伯健太郎　Kentaro Shihaku
P=青山たかかず　Takakazu Aoyama
SB=電通　DENTSU Inc.

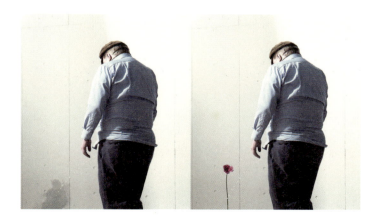

花がないのとあるのでは世界は こんなに違うことを示すポスター

花に対して、日常的に意識の低い人々に向け、花があるのと
ないのでは180度世界がチェンジするという花の力を伝えた。
同じ構図の写真を左右に並べ、花の有無を比較。

A poster that shows the difference between a world with flowers and one without

Directed at people who usually take little notice of flowers, this
poster highlights the power of flowers by showing how the
world would be completely different without them.
Photographs with the same basic composition are displayed on
the left and right, enabling the viewer to compare the same
scene with and without flowers.

マクドナルド リニューアルオープン告知ポスター
McDonald's Renewal Opening Announcement Poster

飲食店 Restaurant | Denmark

CL＝McDonald's
CD＝Poul Mikkelsen
AD＋P＝Mikkel Møller
AD＋P＝Tim Ustrup
SB＝DDB Denmark

ポスター Poster

McDonald's in Birkerød re-opens in 3 weeks

McDonald's in Birkerød re-opens in 2 weeks

54

建設重機と工具でロゴを
再現したリニューアルオープンを
知らせるポスター

いつ再開店するのか絶えず消費者が意識するように、
3週の間、1週ごとに工事がどれぐらい進んでいるか、
ローカルエリアとメディアに露出。建設現場の建設重機や
工具でマクドナルドのロゴを再現した。

A poster announcing the reopening of a
restaurant after refurbishment with the logo
recreated using construction machinery and tools

Displayed in the local area and in local media every week for three weeks to
let consumers know how the construction work was progressing and ensure
people remained aware of the planned reopening date. The McDonald's logo
was recreated using heavy machinery, tools, and other items from the
construction site.

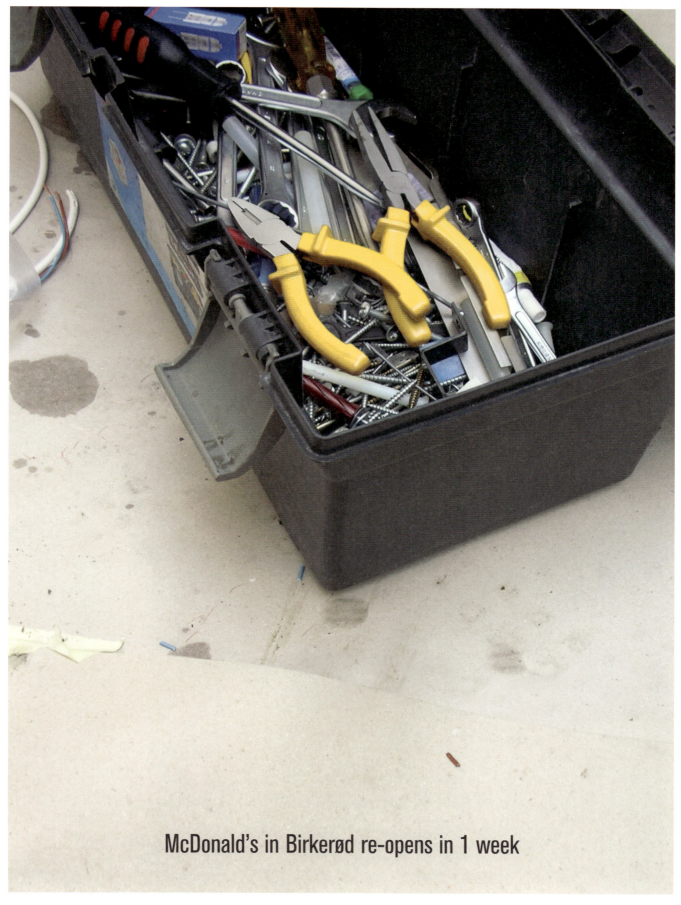

McDonald's in Birkerød re-opens in 1 week

DHL Express ブランディングポスター
DHL Express Branding Poster

配送サービス Courier Service ｜ UK

CL＝DHL Express
AD＋D＝Adam Staples
AD＋D＝Paul Miles
P＝Paul Murphy
SB＝Ogilvy & Mather, London

ポスター　Poster

どんな困難な状況でも必ず荷物を
届ける国際宅配便のポスター

送り先が海に浮かぶ孤島でもアジアの喧騒に巻き込まれても
必ず荷物を届ける。蓋の開いたマンホール、橋の上に揃えら
れた衣服と靴など状況だけを提示し、配達人の姿は見せずに
想像力を膨らます余地を残した。

Posters for an international courier service that delivers without fail no matter how difficult the circumstances

Delivers without fail even if the recipient is on an isolated island in the middle of the ocean or caught up in the tumult of Asia. The advertisement leaves room for the imagination by indicating just the circumstances, such as an open manhole cover or clothing and shoes arranged on top of a bridge, and not showing the actual delivery person.

Perdua Myvi Fast Enough 〝地震、津波〟商品販促ポスター
Perdua Myvi Fast Enough "Earthquqke, Tsunami" Product Promotion Poster

自動車メーカー Automobile Manufacturer｜Malaysia

CL＝Perodua Sales Malaysia
CD＝Ted Lim
AD＝Lee Kah Shing
AD＝Chow Kok Keong
P＝Brandon Wong (STUDIO ROM)
SB＝Naga DDB Malaysia

危険を目前にしても余裕で記念写真を撮るという表現で自動車の性能をアピールしたポスター

自動車のスピードを、危険を目前にしながら記念写真を撮る余裕で示した連作ポスター。地震や津波、竜巻が目前に迫っても、すばやく走り去ることができるので、いつでも逃げ出せる十分な時間があると表現した。

A series of posters for an automobile that show the driver stopping to take photographs even in the face of danger

A series of posters that emphasize an automobile's speed by showing the driver relaxed enough to take photographs even in the face of impending danger. The posters show that even with such dangers as an earthquake, tsunami, and tornado bearing down on him, because he can drive away quickly, the driver has enough time to take photographs and still manage to escape.

SANYO AQUA 商品販促ポスター
SANYO AQUA Product Promotion Poster

家電メーカー House Electronics Manufacturer │ Japan

CL＝三洋電機 SANYO Electric Co., Ltd.
CD＝岩井伸之祐 Shinnosuke Iwai
AD＝鈴木克彦 Katsuhiko Suzuki
D＝小塚泰彦 Yasuhiko Kozuka
D＝土肥純一朗 Junichiro Dohi
CW＝安谷滋元 Jigen Yasutani
CW＝窪田健美 Takemi Kubota
P＝西田宗之 Muneyuki Nishida
CG＝村山輝代 Teruyo Murayama
DF＝ツインズ TWINS CO., LTD.
SB＝博報堂 HAKUHODO INC.

煙や菌などの目に見えない汚れまで洗える洗濯機の機能を表現

空気（オゾン）で洗える洗濯機が出たことを
伝えるために、煙や菌などの目に見えない汚れを
除菌、消臭する機能を煙の服で表現。
ありとあらゆる煙の素材を撮影し、
イメージに近いフォルムを探って制作した。

A poster for a washing machine that uses smoke in the shape of various items of clothing to represent stains

In order to advertise the fact that washing machines
that clean using ozone are now available, the ability
of such machines to disinfect and deodorize stains
caused by such things as smoke and bacteria that are
invisible to the naked eye is represented by smoke in
the shape of various items of clothing. The effect was
created by photographing all kinds of smoke and
looking for shapes close to those the designer had in
mind.

Jewelry Scarabe ブランディングポスター
Jewelry Scarabe Branding Poster

アパレル Apparel｜Japan

CL＝スカラベ Scarabe
CD＋AD＋D＝えぐちりか Rika Eguchi
CW＝磯島拓矢 Takuya Isojima
CW＝古市景子 Keiko Furuichi
P＝青山たかかず Takakazu Aoyama
S＝丸本達彦 Tatsuhiko Marumoto

Hairmake＝HIROTAKA
CG＝張替 誠 Makoto Harikae
Printing Director＝太田正穂 Masaho Ota
DF＝アマナ amana inc.
SB＝電通 DENTSU INC.

ポスター　Poster

WEAR JEALOUSY.

JEWELRY S CARABE

60

ジュエリーを身につけているという優越感を、指のシワを顔に見立てることで表現

ジュエリーからもたらされるジェラシーや虚栄心といった心の内側の本音を、指のシワを顔に見立ててシニカルに描くことで、ブランドの魅力を個性的にウィット豊かに表現した。

In-store advertising for a jewelry brand that creates brand presence.

Expresses in a distinctive and witty way the appeal of the brand concerned by cynically portraying the true feelings of jealousy and vanity stirred up by jewelry, likening the wrinkles on fingers to a face.

GUINNESS〝ボトルの錯覚〟ブランディングポスター、マッチ
GUINNESS "Bottle Illusion" Branding Poster, Pint Matchbook

飲料品メーカー Beverage Manufacturer │ U.S.A

CL＝GUINNESS
CD＝Gerry Graf
AD＋SB＝Frank Anselmo
AD＝Jayson Atienza
P＝Mike Wilson
DF＝BBDO

ポスター Poster

誰もが知るパブでのパイント売り
黒ビールのイメージを利用した広告

黒いビールとクリーミィな泡というギネスの一番有名なイメージを利用。
空のパイントグラスの間にできた空間がボトルの形になっている。
マッチは黒い軸と白い火薬がパイントグラスに入ったギネスの形を模している。

An advertisement that uses a familiar image of a dark beer sold by the pint in pubs

Uses the most famous image of Guinness, a dark beer with creamy froth.
The space inside the empty pint glass is the shape of a bottle. The matches
with their black sticks and white heads also resemble Guinness in a pint glass.

61

味の素〝パルスイート〟商品販促ポスター
AJINOMOTO "Pal Sweet" Product Promotion Poster

食料品メーカー Foodstuff Manufacturer │ Japan

CL=味の素 AJINOMOTO CO., INC.
CD＋AD=井貫大士 Daiji Inuki
D=大矢憲生 Norio Ohya (a)
D=上杉麻実 Asami Uesugi (a)
D=近藤 薫 Kaoru Kando (b, c)
D=工藤隆雅 Takamasa Kudo (c)
CW=野原 均 Hitoshi Nohara (a, b, c)
CW=渋谷三紀 Miki Shibuya (a)

P=和田 恵 Megumu Wada (a)
P=新藤修一 Shuichi Shindo (c)
P=武内俊明 Toshiaki Takeuchi (b)
CG=新井 卓 Takashi Arai (a)
CG=福岡 修 Osamu Fukuoka (b, c)
DF=サン SUN Co., Ltd (a)
DF=グリップ Grip, Inc. (b, c)
SB=アサツーディ・ケイ ASATSU - DK INC.

a

ユーモアたっぷりに消費者に訴求する ダイエタリー甘味料のポスター

『スイッチ篇』では〝カロリーOFFにカラダを切り替えましょう〟というコンセプトから、スイッチのON／OFFとおなかのでっぱりのギミックを使用。『指輪篇』では夫婦の幸せ太りで結婚指輪が裂けるぐらい太るバカバカしさ、『ガラスの靴篇』では重くてガラスの靴のかかとが折れたシンデレラを連想させることで、ダイエタリー甘味料パルスイートの必要性をアピールした。

A poster for a dietary sweetener that uses a strong dose of humor to appeal to consumers

The "switch" version is based on the concept of changing one's appearance dramatically by reducing one's calorie intake and relies on a gimmick involving an ON/OFF switch and a protruding stomach.
The "ring" version promotes the dietary sweetener Pal Sweet by presenting a ridiculous situation in which a couple happily putting on weight to the point where their wedding rings break, while the "glass slipper" version portrays Cinderella so heavy the heel of her glass slipper breaks.

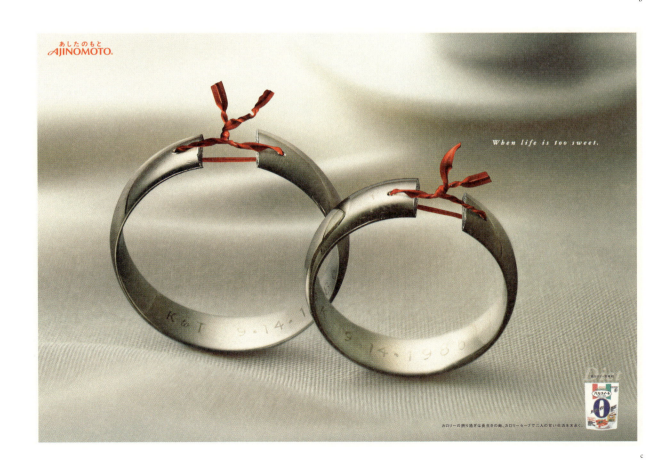

63

b

c

東急ハンズ銀座店オープン告知新聞広告
Tokyu Hands Ginza Store Open Announcement Newspaper Advertisement

日用品メーカー Commodity Manufacturer │ Japan

CL＝東急ハンズ Tokyu Hands
AD＋D＋SB＝吉田ユニ Yuni Yoshida
P＝今元秀明 Hideaki Imamoto

東急ハンズ銀座店オープンのロゴを
実際に店内で売られている
商品を使って制作

3人のアーティストが東急ハンズに売っている物を使い、
ロゴを制作するという新聞5段広告の企画の中の1つ。
毛糸と女の子を使い、ロゴを再現した。実際に毛糸をまいたロゴを作り、
女の子の服を同じ毛糸を作って真上から撮影した。

A newspaper advertisement for the
opening of Tokyu Hands' Ginza store that
uses actual products

One of three proposals that involved three artists using products sold
at Tokyu Hands to recreate the store's logo. In this case the artist
used woolen yarn and a girl to recreate the logo. The actual logo was
made by winding the wool. The girl's clothes were made using the
same wool and the scene photographed from directly overhead.

リカクチュール店頭ブランディングポスター
"riccacouture" In-store Branding Poster

アパレル Apparel │ Japan

CL＝リカクチュール riccacouture
AD＋D＝永松りょうこ Ryoko Nagamatsu

桃をお尻に見立ててかわいらしく 表現した下着の店頭ポスター

下着は女性の肌を守るもの。桃でお尻を象徴するのは
一般的なので、そこに下着をつけたらカワイイと思い制作した。
梱包用のスチロールをショーツ型にし、実物の桃にはかせた。

A shop-window poster for women's underwear designed to protect the body that uses a peach to represent the buttocks

Underwear is designed to protect a woman's body. Using a peach to represent the buttocks is commonplace, so for added cuteness the peach was clothed in underwear. Packaging styrene was shaped into a pair of shorts which were then put on a real peach.

秋のオーダー会告知ポスター
The fitting session in autumn Announcement Poster

アパレル Apparel │ Japan

CL＝ディコ Dico
AD＋D＝永松りょうこ Ryoko Nagamatsu
D＝内田雅之 Masayuki Uchida

洋服の美しいパターンを 利用してタイポグラフィとした こだわりのポスター

アパレルの秋のオーダー会のポスター。
服のパターンそのものの形が美しかったことから、
洋服のパターンを構成してタイポグラフィを作成し、
オーダー会に来る顧客にパターンへのこだわりを伝えた。

A poster that uses typography made up of dressmaking patterns

A poster for an apparel company's fall fitting session. The shapes of the patterns themselves were so beautiful it was decided to create typography made up of dressmaking patterns, a move that also conveyed to customers attending the fitting session how important patterns are to the company.

CL＝バーニベット BERNIVET
AD＋D＝角南貴雅 Takamasa Sunami
CW＝松尾美貴子 Mikiko Matsuo
P＝マーク・ヴァサーロ Mark Vassallo
Retouching＝中村大寿 Hirotoshi Nakamura
DF＋SB＝マック東京 MAQ inc. TOKYO

ポスター Poster

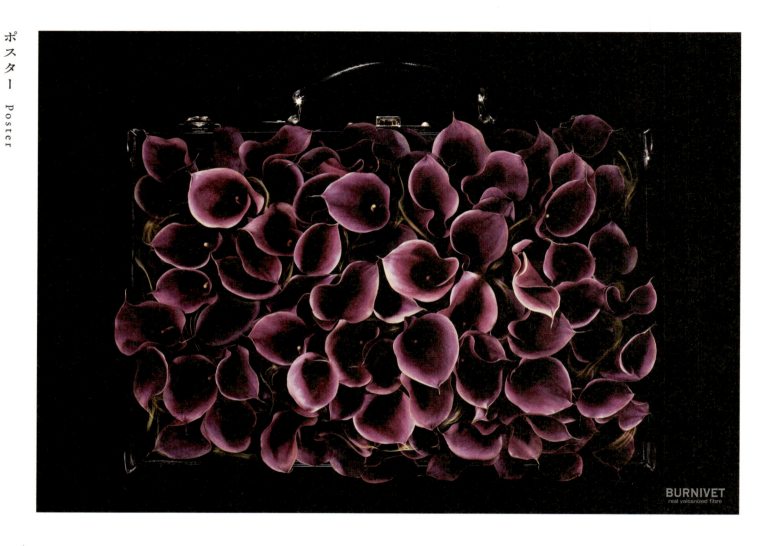

66

〝オーラ〟を〝燃える〟視覚的アナロジーとして表現した旅行鞄のポスター

持つ人の感性や存在感を高めてくれるような商品イメージを伝える
高級旅行鞄の連作ポスター。優美なイメージのカラーの花と、
旅の自由さのシンボルとして世界中の蝶とを製品の存在と重ね合わせ、
妖艶な存在感を表現。

A poster for a travel bag that relies on a visual analogy of an "aura" and "burning"

A series of posters for a luxury travel bag that conveys the product's image of
increasing the owner's sensitivity and presence. A captivating presence was expressed
by superimposing flowers in colors that have a refined image and butterflies from
around the world symbolizing the freedom of travel over the actual product.

b+ad ブランディングポスター
b+ab Branding Poster

アパレル Apparel ｜ Japan

CL=アイティ アパレルズ リミテッド／ビープラスエービー I.T apparels limited／b+ab
AD+D+SB=吉田ユニ　Yuni Yoshida
D=山根恵美　Emi Yamane
P=内田将二　Shoji Uchida

〝いつもの視点を変えてみて！〟という
メッセージを込めて真下から撮影された
アパレルメーカーのポスター

主に中国で展開する香港のアパレルメーカーの秋冬広告。
いつもの視点を変えてみるという発想から、女の子の部屋を真下から
みた構図になった。本物の動物を使用し、強化ガラスの床のセットを
作り真下から撮影。

A poster for an apparel manufacturer
shot from directly below to present a
different angle

The fall-winter advertisement for a Hong Kong apparel manufacturer most
of whose products are sold in China. Based on the idea of presenting a
different angle on things, the poster shows a girl's room shot from directly
below. Real animals were used, and a set with a toughened glass floor was
built to shoot the scene in the poster.

67

〝地獄〟チリソース商品販促ポスター
"Hell" Chili Sauce Product Promotion Poster

食料品メーカー Foodstuff Manufacturer｜Germany

CL＝Figueroa Brothers, Inc.
CD＝Buchhart von Scheven
CD＝Stephan Gauser
AD＝Christian Bobst
CW＝Jan Harbeck
CW＝Micho Stolz
I＝Paul Roberts
Account＝Heuning Gerstuer
SB＝Jung von Matt AG

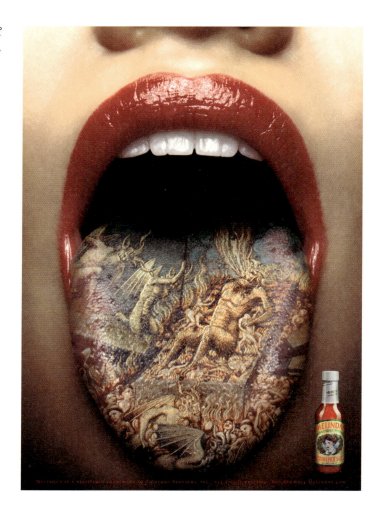

炎で焼かれるほど辛いことを
地獄絵図を利用して表現

ハラペーニョを使った激辛ソースで知られる食品メーカーが展開した
連作ポスター。女性の舌で繰り広げられるおぞましい光景は、
フラ・アンジェリコや、ハンス・メムリンクらが15世紀に描いた
地獄の図を使用した。

A poster for a chili sauce so hot it's like being burned in hellfire that borrows from famous paintings

A series of posters developed by a food manufacturer known for its fiery hot sauce made using jalapeno peppers. The horrific scenes that unfold on the woman's tongue draw on the depictions of hell by such 15th century artists as Fra Angelico and Hans Memling.

Splenda 商品案内ポスター
Splenda Product Promotion Poster

食料品メーカー Foodstuff Manufacturer │ Peru

CL＝Johnson & Johnson
CD＝Ricardo Mares
CD＝Mauricio Fernandez
SB＝McCann Erickson Corp. Publicidad S. A.

〝甘いものを恐れるな！〟
ケーキをワニやモンスターに見立てた
人口甘味料のポスター

どんな料理にも使える人口甘味料を使用すれば、
カロリーを気にすることなくものを食べられるようになる。
人口甘味料は食べたくてたまらない甘いものを
食べることが可能にすることを表現した。

"Don't be afraid of sweets!"
A poster for an artificial sweetener

Use this artificial sweetener, which can be added to any kind of
cooking, and you can eat anything without worrying about
calories. Highlights the concept that artificial sweeteners make it
possible for us to eat the sweet things we all crave.

〝トング、ボトム、ティッツ〟キャンペーン
Thong, Bottom, Tits Campaign

出版 Publishing ｜ Spain

CL＝Random house manoadori / debolsillo
CD＝Jaume Mones
CD＋AD＝Francesc Talanino
P＝Garrigosa Studio
SB＝Bassat Oglivy & Mather

女性の水着の日焼けあとを連想させる
〝この夏は本を読もう！〟キャンペーン

夏の刺激的なレッスンをコンセプトに読書の魅力を伝えるポスター。
本のページに映り込む影の曲線が女性の水着の日焼けあとを思わせ、
シンプルだが、魅力的なデザインで好奇心をかきたてる。

"Read a book this summer" campaign that reminisce of the tan lineson a female figure

A poster that conveys the appeal of books based on the concept of exciting summer lessons. The curves of the shadow cast on the page of the book are reminiscent of the tan lines on a female figure, and the poster piques the curiosity with its simple yet appealing design.

Love passport a bloom 〝Honeybee〟ブランディングポスター
Love passport a bloom "Honeybee" Branding Poster

化粧品メーカー　Cosmetic Manufacturer │ Japan

CL＝フィッツコーポレーション　Fits Corporation K.K.
CD＋AD＝新開宏明　Hiroaki Shinkai
AD＋D＝谷野一矢　Kazuya Tanino
CW＝笹島真祐子　Mayuko Sasajima
P＝坂本アキラ　Akira Sakamoto
SB＝ジェイ・ダブル・ティ・ジャパン　JWT Japan

群がるミツバチで香水が
〝多くの人々を魅了する花の香り〟で
あることを伝えるポスター

香水をつけた部分に群がる蜜蜂をリアルに
表現することで、香水が〝多くの人々を引きつけて魅了
する花の香り〟であることをユニークに伝える。

A poster informing people that a
fragrance has "a floral scent that
appeals to many people"

By realistically portraying honeybees swarming over the part of the poster
scented with the fragrance, the designers likened the allure of the fragrance to
'the scent of flowers that attracts countless male bees,' thereby communicating
the idea that the fragrance has 'a floral scent that appeals to many people'.

Breaded Faces 商品案内ポスター
Breaded Faces Product Promotion Poster

電気メーカー Electronics Manufacturer ｜ Germany

CL＝Payer Germany GmbH
CD＝Matthias Spaetgens
CD＝Jan Leube
AD＝Johannes Hicks
AD＝Mathias Rebmann
P＝Hans Starck
CW＝Stuart Kummer
Postproduction＝Appel Grafik Berlin
SB＝Scholz & Friends Berlin

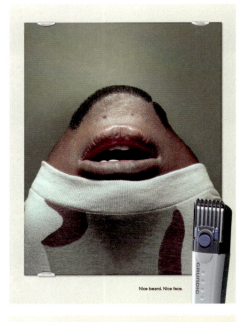

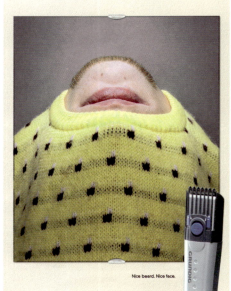

顔をさかさまにして髪型に見立て、個性ある髭の大切さをアピール

ブランドの浸透を目的とした男性向け、髭用トリマーの広告。
手入れした髭は個性を特徴づけるものだと認識させるため、
顔を上下逆にし、整えた髭がそれぞれ髪型に見えるようにして、
髭の重要性を表現した。

A beard trimmer advertisement that highlights the importance of facial hair by turning faces upside down

An advertisement for a men's beard trimmer that aims at brand penetration. In order to raise awareness of the role well-trimmed facial hair plays in expressing one's individuality, faces are turned upside down so that various facial hairstyles look like different hairdos, thereby stressing the importance of facial hair.

ギャツビーヘアワックス商品案内ポスター
GATSBY Hair Wax Product Promotion Poster

化粧品メーカー　Cosmetic Manufacturer ｜ Japan

CL＝マンダム　mandom corp.
CD＝辻中達也　Tatsuya Tsujinaka
CD＝山崎隆明　Takaaki Yamazaki
AD＝高木大輔　Daisuke Takagi
D＝古川純也　Junya Furukawa
CW＝山崎英生　Hideo Yamazaki
P＝石川 寛　Hiroshi Ishikawa
Producer＝清水敦之　Atsuyuki Shimizu
DF＝大阪宣伝研究所　Osaka Senden Kenkyusho Co., Ltd.
SB＝電通関西支社　DENTSU Inc. KANSAI

73

〝オス〟のイメージを髪型で
具現化したヘアワックスのポスター

世の中の全ての男性に向けて、ヘアワックスの魅力を
訴求するために、〝オス〟のイメージを髪型で具現化した。
イメージラフを元に3種類の髪型を人毛を使用して成形。
モデルの頭に特殊メイクを施した。

Posters for hair wax with hairstyles that
embody an image of "masculinity"

In order to promote the allure of hair wax to men everywhere, an
image of "masculinity" was embodied using hairstyles. Based on
a rough image, three kinds of hairstyles were created using
human hair. Special makeup was applied to the models' faces.

Sunsilk シャンプー 商品案内ポスター
Sunsilk Shampoo Product Promotion Poster

製薬 Pharmaceuticals | Poland

CL＝Unilever
CD＋P＝Darek Zatorski
AD＝Karolina Czarnota
CW＝Monika Kaminska
SB＝J. Walter Thompson Polska

靴紐の代わりにもなるくらい
丈夫な髪をつくるシャンプーのポスター

製品の使用により、どんなに髪が丈夫になるかを、
真に強い髪は日常生活で使用されている他のものの代わりに
なることで表現。スニーカーの靴紐が1本の髪の毛になっている。

A shampoo advertisement that shows hair strong enough to be used to tie a shoe

Shows just how strong hair will become if the product is used by showing really strong hair being used in place of other things in everyday situations. A lace on a sneaker is replaced with a single strand of hair.

Poett Bosque, Poett Mar エアフレッシュナー商品案内ポスター
Poett Bosque, Poett Mar Air Freshener Product Promotion Poster

日用品メーカー Commodity Manufacturer │ Chile

CL＝Clorox Chile
CD＝Jorge Leiva
AD＝Victor Mora
SB＝DDB CHILE S.A.

ポスター Poster

75

ひと吹きで森や海へといざなう
エアフレッシュナー

ほんの少しの香りが、すばらしい場所へと連れて行ってくれる
というコンセプトで、製品の独自の芳香を伝えた。
〝単純さ〟〝驚き〟〝笑顔〟が制作アイデアの基本となっている。

An advertisement for an air freshener that beckons people to the forest or the sea with a single whiff

Conveys an impression of the unique fragrance of the product based on the concept of the faintest of scents transporting people to a wonderful place. "Simplicity," "surprise," and "a smile" formed the basis of the creative process.

Siemens 〝掃除婦〟キャンペーン
Siemens Charlady Campaign

家電メーカー Home Electronics Manufacturer │ Germany

CL=BSH Bosch und Siemens
CL=Hacsgeraete GmBH
CD=Stefan Setzkorn
CD=Silke Schneider
CD=Gunnar Loeser
AD=Alex Schilling

AD=Marc Ebenwaldner
CW=Johan H. Ohlson
CW=Alexandar Schierl
Graphics=Pia Schneider
P=hiepler, brunier,
SB=Scholz & Friends Humburg

Der leiseste Staubsauger seiner Klasse: technopower sound & silence.   Siemens. Die Zukunft zieht ein.

ありえない状況で掃除機を使用し 静音機能を強調するポスター

高い静音機能が売りの掃除機の連作ポスター。オペラコンサート、
教会での結婚式など、最も雑音を嫌うシチュエーションで製品を使用しても、
だれも気に留めないことで音が静かなことを表現した。

A poster for a vacuum cleaner that emphasizes its noise-reduction properties by showing it being used in unlikely situations

A series of posters for a vacuum cleaner whose selling point is its
superior noise-reduction function. The quietness was emphasized
by hinting that no one would mind even if the product were used
in situations where noise is most unwelcome, such as a chess
tournament, an opera concert, and a church wedding.

Marbels〝バス、船、列車〞商品案内ポスター
Marbels - Bus, Ship, Train Product Promotion Poster

菓子製造・販売 Confectionaries Manufacturer, Sales │ India

CL＝Perfetti Van Melle   AD＝Ravi Shanker
ECD＝Piyush Pandey   CW＝Avinash Baliga
CD＝Abhijit Avasthi   P＝Corbis
CD＝Manoj Shetty   P＝Getty Editorial
CD＝Siddhartha Dutta   SB＝Ogilvy & Mather, India

中身がぎっしり詰まっていることを
表現した360個入りキャンディの広告

パッケージに360個ものキャンディが入っていることを
強調するために、人々がぎっしりとバスや船に
乗り込んでいる画像を使用したプリントや屋外広告を通して、
パッケージの中がどれほど詰まっているかを伝えた。

An advertisement for candy that
comes in packages of 360 designed to
encourage impulsive buying

Shows how full each package is through print and outdoor
advertisements using images of people crammed into busses and boats in
order to emphasize the fact that each package contains 360 candies.

ANA〝旅割〟告知ポスター
ANA "Tabi - Wari" Announcement Poster

航空 Airline ｜ Japan

CL＝全日本空輸 All Nippon Airways
CD＝白石大介 Daisuke Shiraishi
AD＝鈴木克彦 Katsuhiko Suzuki
D＝角南貴雅 Takamasa Sunami
D＝柿崎裕生 Yusei Kakizaki
D＝岸田麻里 Mari Kishida
CW＝伊東 毅 Takeshi Ito
P＝薄井一議 Kazuyoshi Usui
DF＝博報堂 HAKUHODO INC.
DF＋SB＝マック東京 MAQ inc. TOKYO

ポスター Poster

旅行を身近に、
日常化してもらうことを目的にした
航空会社のキャンペーン

〝日常から非日常へ〟旅行の楽しさを表現するために、
日常生活の中でよく見かける標識、エレベーター、信号、
階段等のピクトグラムが旅に出かけるという設定で、
シンボリックにグラフィックを展開した。

An airline company campaign that
aimed to make travel a more familiar,
everyday experience

In order to convey the joy of travel as a journey "from the
everyday to the non-everyday," the graphics were developed
symbolically based on the premise of pictograms of things we
often see during our day-to-day lives such as signs, elevators,
signals, and stairs going on holiday.

DFS沖縄〝買うたのしみは、すべてに勝る〟ブランディングポスター
DFS Galleria Okinawa "Shopping wins over all desires" Branding Poster

商業施設 Commercial Facility｜Japan

CL＝DFS ギャラリア・沖縄 DFS GALLERIA OKINAWA
CD＝市野沢茂彦 Shigehiko Ichinosawa
CD＋CW＝福田英彦 Hidehiko Fukuda
AD＝荻原正樹 Masaki Ogiwara
D＝金福順 Kim Poksun
P＝坂本アキラ Akira Sakamoto
Producer＝星本和容 Kazuhiro Hoshimoto
SB＝オグルヴィ・ワン・ジャパン、広告堂 Ogilvy One Japan, KOUKOKUDO

買い物に夢中だったことを
日焼けのかたちで
ストレートに伝えたポスター

女性の日焼けしていない部分をよく見ると、
ショッピングバッグの形をしており、
買い物に夢中だったことが判る仕掛けになっている屋外広告。
日焼けは本物で日焼けしていない白い肌の加工をした。

Posters for DFS Okinawa that communicates in a straightforward manner "the joy of shopping"

If you look closely at the area of the woman's body that isn't tanned on this outdoor advertisement you'll see it resembles the shape of a shopping bag, suggesting she was too busy shopping to do anything else. The suntan is real, while the untanned area of white skin has been retouched.

Ocean Basket Seafood Restaurant 〝フィッシュアンドチップス〟新聞広告
Ocean Basket Seafood Restaurant "Fish & Chips" Newspaper Advertisement

飲食店 Restaurant ｜ South Africa

CL＝Ocean Basket
CD＝Liezl-Mari Long
AD＝Brendan Hoffmann
AD＝Lucas van Vuuren
D＝NA

P＝Pete Maltbie
I＝Paul Hudson
CW＝Hanlie Kriel
CW＝Jonathan Warncke
DF＋SB＝Joe Public South Africa

できたてのフィッシュアンドチップスの ような新聞の全面広告

フィッシュアンドチップスが人気メニューのレストランの新聞広告。
港にあるような地元の小さな店ではフィッシュアンドチップスは
必ず新聞に包まれて売られており、まるでできたてが
目の前にあるかのように表現。

A full-page newspaper ad with what appears to be a freshly cooked serving of fish and chips

A newspaper advertisement for a restaurant where fish and chips is one of
the most popular dishes on the menu. At small, local fish and chip shops
by the seaside, fish and chips are usually sold wrapped in newsprint, so the
advertisement was created to give the reader the impression that a freshly
cooked serving was right there in front of them.

〝南アルプス天然水〟新聞広告
Product Promotion Newspaper Advertisement "South Alps Mineral Water"

飲料品メーカー Beverage Manufacturer │ Japan

CL＝サントリー SUNTORY LIMITED.
CD＝神谷幸之助 Konosuke Kamitani
AD＝河合雄流 Takeru Kawai
DW＝辻野 裕 Yutaka Tsujino
SB＝電通 DENTSU Inc.

自然からできたおいしい水を表現した フラップ状の新聞広告

山に雪が降り、それが地中にしみておいしい水に
なることを、時間の経過と、ちょっとした驚きで伝えようとした。
紙は3枚重なっており、めくると雪景色から春の景色へ、
最後に全面に水が流れ落ちる写真となる。

A fold-out newspaper advertisement that expresses the concept of clean drinking water sourced from nature

This advertisement seeks to convey through the passage of time and a hint
of surprise the concept of snow in the mountains melting and seeping
down into the earth to become clean drinking water. The advertisement is
spread over three pages and consists of photos that portray firstly a snow
scene, then a scene in spring, and finally a full page of cascading water.

Touareg 差し込み広告
Touareg Insert Advertisement

自動車メーカー Automobile Manufacturer｜Brazil

CL＝Volkswagen
CD＝Marcello Serpa
AD＝Roberts Fernandez
CW＝Sophie Schoenburg
Producer＝José Roberts Begewa
SB＝Almap BBDO

カタログ　Catalog

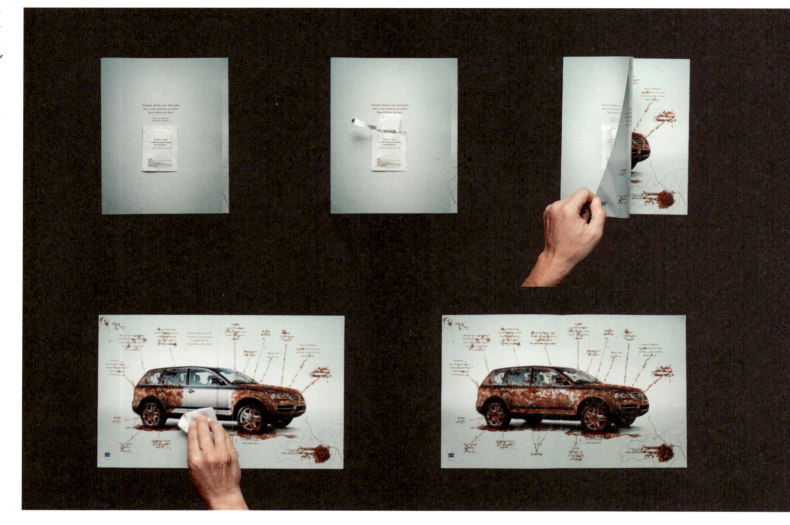

泥に負けない
本格的オフロード性能を
そなえたSUV車のカタログ

フォルクスワーゲン初の高級SUV車トゥアレグの広告。
まるで本物のような泥は、この広告で初めて使用された
特殊ペイント。表紙に付いたティッシュで泥を拭き取ると、
車の外観と機能が明らかになる。

A catalog for an SUV with genuine
off-road capabilities that won't be
beaten by mud

An advertisement for the Tuareg, Volkswagen's first ever luxury
SUV. The almost lifelike mud was produced with special paint
that was used for the first time in this advertisement. A tissue
attached to the cover is used to wipe away the mud revealing a
likeness of the vehicle and details of its features.

Controle
de distância de
estacionamento.

Ar-condicionado
com temperaturas
diferentes
para cada parte
do carro.

Transmissão
automática
de 6 marchas.

Piloto
automático.

Eleito o Melhor
Sport Utility
de luxo do mundo,
pela revista
Motor Trend.

E o mais
surpreendente,
é um Volkswagen.

Faróis
bixênon.

Bancos elétricos
com 12 posições
de aquecimento.

6 airbags.

Motor V8
de 310 cv.

Touareg.
Um absurdo de carro.

CL＝Sixty Group
CD＋AD＝Mauro Pastore
CD＋AD＝Masa Magnoni
CD＋AD＝Alessandro Floridia
D＋P＋I＝Luisa Piras
DF＝Cacao Design
Printing＝Fontegrafica
SB＝Cacao Design

カタログ　Catalog

84

製品イメージが印刷された
シール紙を自由に貼って楽しめる
アパレルカタログ

ターゲット層の年齢を考慮したカタログというより、
インタラクティブなゲームとして受けいれ可能なアパレルカタログ。
シール紙に印刷された製品イメージを剥がし、自由にカタログの
背景に貼ることができる。

An interactive apparel catalog
that presents the product images
in a fresh way

Rather than a catalog designed with the target demographic
in mind, this is an apparel catalog that can be used as an
interactive game. The product images, which are printed on
sticker paper, can be removed and stuck at will on the
background scenes in the catalog.

SAVANDER ブランドカタログ
SAVANDER Branding Catalog

スノーボードブランド Snow Board Brand │ Japan

CL＝ボイジャー リンク VOYAGER LINK LTD.
CD＝石川健二（ボイジャーリンク）Kenji Ishikawa (VOYAGER LINK)
AD＋D＝青井達也 Tatsuya Aoi
DF＋SB＝ノーザン グラフィックス Northern Graphics

星座の早見表のような スノーボードブランドの カタログ

ブランドのイメージを理解してもらいながら新商品を
伝えるため、星座の早見表のような仕様で商品を
見せることができれば面白いと考えた。星座の早見表のように
クルクル回しながら商品をセレクトしていく。

A catalog in the shape of a planisphere for a brand of snowboard

As a way of promoting greater understanding of the brand
image as well introducing new products, it was thought it
would be interesting if the products could be presented in a
way similar to a planisphere. The products are selected by
rotating the catalog like a planisphere.

---

adidas SALMON 商品案内カタログ
adidas SALMON Product Promotion Catalog

スポーツ用品 Sport Goods Brand │ Japan

CL＝アディダス ジャパン adidas Japan K.K.
CD＝小松裕行 Hiroyuki Komatsu
AD＝瀬川洋介 Yosuke Segawa
AD＋DF＝アトリエタイク ateliertaik
D＝臼田香太 Kota Usuda
D＝植草麻奈美 Manami Uekusa
SB＝アトリエタイク ateliertaik co., ltd.

雪山のディスプレイにもなる スキーのトップブランドのカタログ

広げる大きさ、角度が売り場に合わせてフレキシブルに
変化するディスプレイにもなるカタログ。
広げた度合いによって見える山の連なりの形状を計算し、
オリジナルの折りパターンで機械折りと手折りを組み合わせた。

A catalog for a leading ski brand that doubles as a display of snow-covered mountains

A catalog that doubles as a display whose size and angles can be
flexibly altered to suit any sales floor. The catalog was folded
mechanically and by hand according to an original folding pattern
taking into account the shape of the mountains that would be
visible depending on the extent to which the catalog is open.

Cacao Design 会社案内
Cacao Design Brochure

デザイン会社 Design Firm｜Italy

CL＋DF＋SB＝Cacao Design
CD＋AD＝Mauro Pastore
CD＋AD＝Masa Magnoni
CD＋AD＋D＝Alessandro Floridia
P＝Giuseppe Toja (still life)
P＝Claudio Gaiaschi (portraits)
Printing＝Fontegrafica

カタログ　Catalog

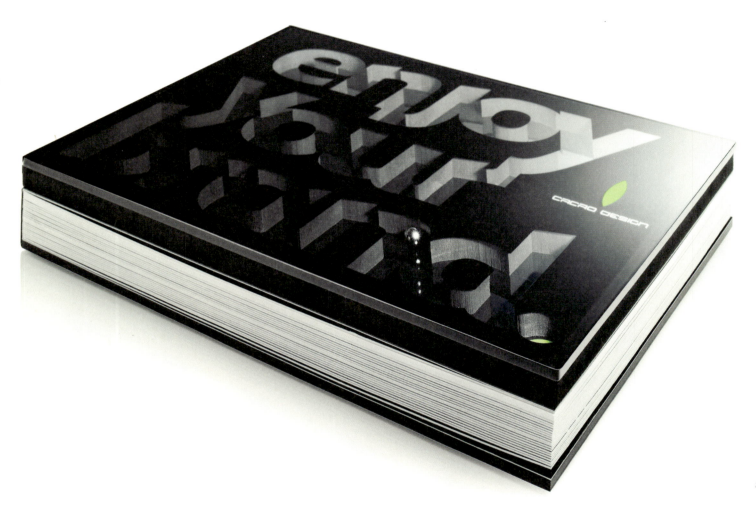

ページをめくりながら楽しめる
デザイン会社のパンフレット

Cacao Designの優れた創造性とすべての製品の
細部までのこだわりを紹介するパンフレット。
すぐに片付けられてしまう他のパンフレットとは違い、
ページをめくりながら楽しめるものとして構成されている。

A pamphlet for a design
company that's a joy to read

A pamphlet that conveys the exceptional creativity and
attention to product detail that are hallmarks of Cacao
Design. Unlike most other pamphlets, which are soon put
away, this pamphlet is designed to be something that the
reader can truly enjoy as they turn the pages.

交差点〝間違った判断は命取り〟カタログ
Intersections - Bad calls can be deadly Catalog

自動車メーカー Automodile Manufacturer｜New Zealand

CL＝Land Transport NZ
CD＝Philip Andrew
CD＋AD＋CW＝Mark Harricks
AD＋CW＝Brigid Alkema
P＝Diederik van Heyningen
Typographer＝Chris Chisnall
SB＝Clemenger BBDO

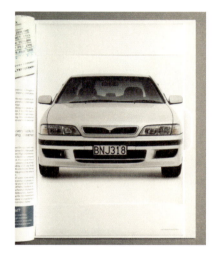  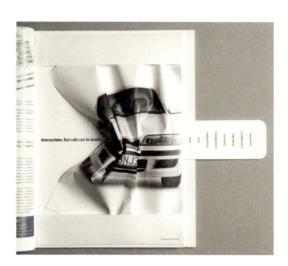

交通死亡事故は交差点でも
発生することを伝える
仕掛けつき雑誌広告

交差点はクラクションを鳴らされるぐらいで比較的安全だと
人々は誤解している。読者が横のつまみをひっぱれば
ひっぱるほど紙がしわくちゃになって車体が歪み、交差点で
側面衝突された車のようになる。

A magazine advertisement with a gimmick
designed to alert drivers to the fact that fatal
traffic accidents also occur at intersections

People mistakenly believe that intersections are so safe that all they need
to do is sound their horn. As the reader pulls the tab on the side, the
paper becomes crumpled and the vehicle body becomes distorted until it
looks just like a vehicle that's been hit from the side at an intersection.

CL＝資生堂ギャラリー Shiseido Gallery
AD＋D＝青木康子 Yasuko Aoki
P＝加藤 健（表紙）Ken Kato (a cover)
DF＋SB＝パンゲア PANGAEA Ltd.

カタログ Catalog

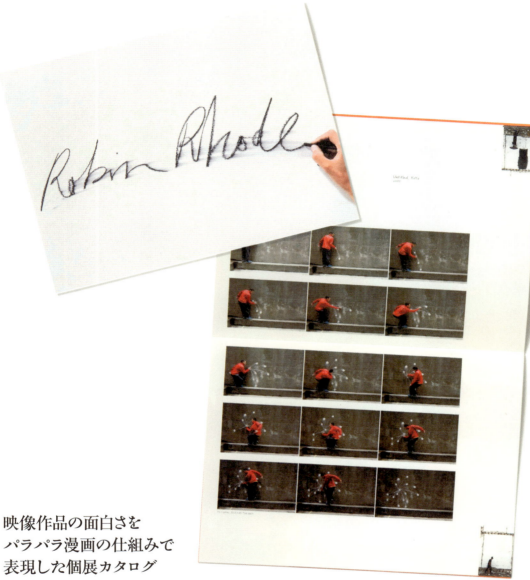

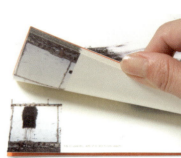

映像作品の面白さを
パラパラ漫画の仕組みで
表現した個展カタログ

インスタレーション作家であるアーティストの
作品のライブ感と動きをカタログでも伝えるため、
ページごとに展開していく作品とは別に、ページの端に、
パラパラ漫画の要領で順番に写真をレイアウトした。

A solo exhibition catalog that uses flip animation to highlight the appeal of video works

In order to convey through the catalog the liveliness and
movement of the work of the artist, who works in the
installation field, in addition to details of the works,
photos were included on the edge of each page of the
catalog in such a way that it also functioned as a flipbook.

〝LIFE〟展 展覧会カタログ
"LIFE" Exhibition Catalog

美術館 Art Museum｜Japan

CL＝水戸芸術館 ART TOWER MITO
D＋SB＝大島依提亜 Idea Oshima
P＝富田里美 Satomi Tomita

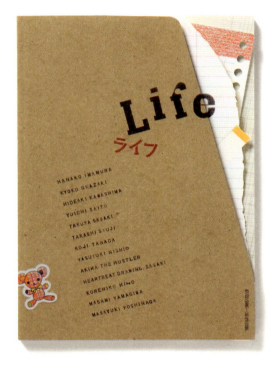

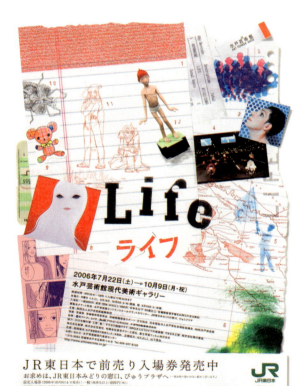

机上の紙の束のような
展覧会カタログ

水戸芸術館〝LIFE〟展のカタログ。〝LIFE〟とは〝人生〟
〝生活〟という広くも狭くもとれる言葉。一個人の机上に
無造作に置かれた紙の束から、〝生活〟が果ては〝人生〟が
垣間見られるような観点から着想した。

A catalog for the LIFE exhibition that
conveys the gist of the show by
resembling a pile of paper on a desk

A catalog for the LIFE exhibition at Art Tower Mito. The word
"life" can be interpreted broadly or narrowly to mean either a
"lifetime" or a "lifestyle." The idea of producing a catalog that
resembles a pile of paper casually placed on someone's desk
came about because it hints at both a "lifestyle" and a "lifetime".

Settimane Musicali 〝音楽週間〟プログラム
Settimane Musicali "Weeks of Music" Program

音楽 Music │ Italy

CL＝Settimane Musicali
CD＋AD＋D＝Massimo Breda
CD＋AD＝Monica Brugnera
DF＝Studio Grafico Fez
SB＝Studio Grafico Fez snc

差し込まれた楽器のカードが
カクテル・パーティの
招待状となるコンサートプログラム

コンサートシーズンのプログラム小冊子。ひじ掛けいすが
楽器へと変身する。楽器はプログラムから取り外すことができ、
実はコンサートの後のカクテル・パーティーへの
招待状となっている。

A concert program in which musical instruments become cocktail party invitations

A concert season program in booklet form. Armchairs are transformed into musical instruments. The instruments can be removed from the program and used as invitations to a cocktail party after the concert.

ピアノ発表会 プログラム
Program for piano concert

音楽教室 Music School ｜ Japan

CL=香雪会　KAYUKI Group
AD＋SB=長嶋りかこ　Rikako Nagashima
D=水溜友絵　Tomoe Mizutamari
P=青山たかかず　Takakazu Aoyama

ピアノの鍵盤をリアルに再現した
ピアノ発表会のプログラム

膝の上で演奏曲を練習した自身の思い出から発想し、
子どもたちが発表会で緊張しないでいつでも弾けるよう
ピアノ鍵盤をプログラムにした。白い鍵盤はマットPP加工、
黒い鍵盤はバーコ印刷で鍵盤をリアルに再現した。

A program for a piano recital that
realistically recreates a piano keyboard

Inspired by the designer's own memories of practicing pieces for a
piano recital on their knees, the decision was made to make a program
in the shape of a piano keyboard so that the children could practice at
any time during the recital without getting nervous. A keyboard was
realistically recreated using matte polypropylene laminate for the
white keys and thermographic printing for the black keys.

91

Haat 2008年 春夏カタログ
Haat 2008 Spring / Summer Catalog

アパレル Apparel｜Japan

CL＝イッセイミヤケ ISSEY MIYAKE INC.
AD＝高井 薫 Kaoru Takai
D＝引地摩里子 Mariko Hikichi
P＝ケイ・オガタ Kei Ogata
Stylist＝広田 聡 Satoshi Hirota
Hair Make＝加茂克也 Katsuya Kamo
SB＝サン・アド Sun-Ad Co., Ltd.

アイテムの様々な表情が楽しめる アパレルブランドのヴィジュアルブック

一見すると、普通のカタログだが、モデルやアイテムが飛び出す
絵本のようにポップアップするアパレルブランドのヴィジュアルブック。
折り込みの部分を開くことで、カタログサイズよりモデルや服が
大きく見える仕掛け。

A visual book for an apparel brand that enables readers to enjoy the various different looks of the items

A visual book for an apparel brand that at first glance looks like a normal
catalog, but that actually features models and items that pop up from the page,
thereby giving readers a better idea of the various looks available. The inserted
sections are cutouts and their position changes from page to page.

Erotic 展覧会カタログ
Erotic Exhibition Catalog

通信、出版 Communications, Publishing ｜ Austria

CL＝Wienbibliothek
CD＋AD＝Cordula Alessandri
D＝Hans Proschofsky
P＝Claudio Alessadri
Production＝Schulteswien
SB＝alessandri design

93

〝エロティック〟展の ジッパー付き展覧会カタログ

ウィーン市立歴史博物館の展覧会カタログ。
厚みのあるプラスティックのカバーのジッパーを開くと
カタログの表紙が現れる。表紙には開閉できる小窓があり、
中には〝調和への試み〟という展覧会の副題が書いてある。

A catalog with a zipper for the "Erotic exhibition"

An exhibition catalog for the Historical Museum of the City of Vienna. The zipper on the thick plastic cover is opened to reveal the catalog cover. On the cover is a small window that can be opened and closed, and inside is written the exhibition subtitle, "An Experiment in Harmony."

ブライトリング クリスマスカード
Breitling Christmas Card

時計輸入販売 Watch Import Maker｜Japan

CL＝ブライトリング・ジャパン BREITLING JAPAN
CD＝宮田 識 Satoru Miyata
CD＋CW＝広瀬正明 Masaaki Hirose
AD＝古屋友章 Tomoaki Furuya
D＝赤木泰隆 Yasutaka Akagi
DF＋SB＝ドラフト DRAFT Co., Ltd.

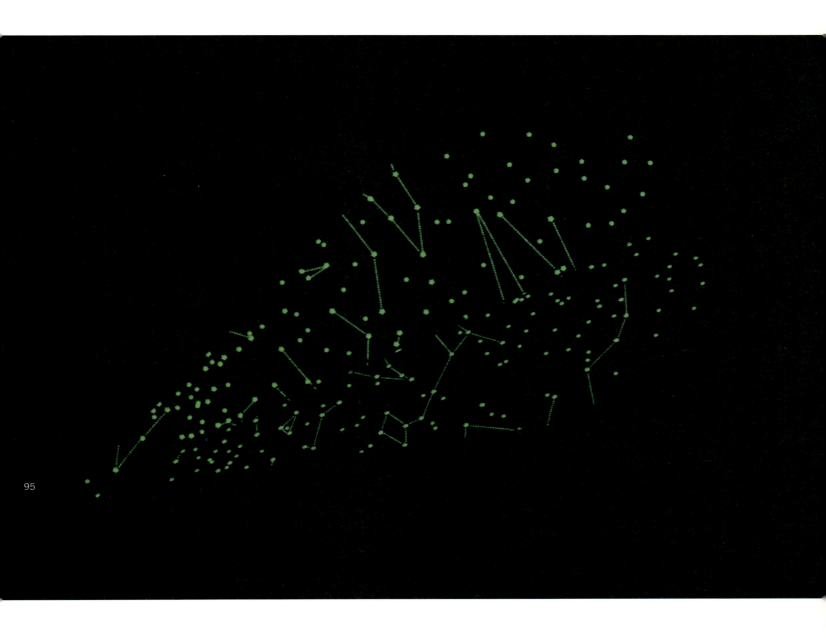

95

機械式腕時計ブランドの
世界を体感してもらうための
クリスマスカード

時計は宇宙の動きを顕在化したもので、ブライトリングは
プロのパイロットのための時計ブランドでもある。
空に近い存在であるブランドの世界を、夜空と飛行機を
モチーフとした蓄光印刷で表現した。

A Christmas card that gives people a taste of the world of a luxury mechanical wristwatch brand

Watches are connected with the movement of the heavens,
and Breitling watches are used by professional pilots. This
glow-in-the-dark Christmas card uses night sky and airplane
motifs to portray the world of a brand with a close
connection to the sky.

"JEWEL GRAPHY" カード
"JEWEL GRAPHY" Card

プロダクトブランド Product Brand｜Japan

CL＝ディーブロス D-BROS
CD＝宮田 識 Satoru Miyata
AD＋D＝福岡南央子 Naoki Fukuoka
SB＝ドラフト DRAFT Co., Ltd.

ダイレクトメール Direct Mail

きらめく紙の宝石を ネックレスにした グリーティングカード

きらめく宝石を平面にして気軽に買えるものにした
グリーティングカード。紙をはと目でとめることで、
ネックレスのような可動性を与え、
たたんで封筒にしまえるようにした。

A greeting card consisting of a necklace made out of glittering paper jewels

A greeting card that transforms glittering jewels
into something that can be bought readily by
presenting them in 2D. The card was given the
movability of a necklace by fastening the paper
with eyelets and was also designed so that it could
be folded and put into an envelope.

アソート クッキーカード 〝Buono Buono〟
Assort Cookie Card "Buono Buono"

デザイン会社 Design Firm │ Japan

CL=ディー・ブロス D-BROS
CD=宮田 識 Satoru Miyata
AD+D=御代田尚子 Naoko Miyoda
Producer=中岡美奈子 Minako Nakaoka
DF+SB=ドラフト DRAFT Co., Ltd.

97

まるで本物のクッキーを
積み重ねたようなグリーティングカード

山盛りのクッキーそのものをグリーティングカードにというアイデアを
出発点に、一枚ものに空押、半切、型抜の加工を施して作成。
メッセージは中面に書いたり、レースペーパーに書いてクッキーの間に
挟んだりと工夫次第でいろいろと使うことができる。お菓子袋のような
白い封筒に入れて、定型内80円で送ることができる。

A greeting card that looks as if
real cookies have been piled up

Originating from the idea of making a greeting card
consisting of actual cookies piled up, this card was made
using blind embossing, scoring, and die-cutting processes.
The sender can write a message on the back of the card, put
it in a white envelope like a bakery bag, and mail it using
an 80-yen stamp.

TIME & STYLE クリスマスカード
TIME & STYLE Chiristmas Card

インテリア　Home Furnishings ｜ Japan

CL＋CD＋SB＝タイム アンド スタイル　TIME & STYLE
I＝永野敬子　Keiko Nagano

〝TIME & STYLE MIDTOWN〟オープン告知DM、ショップカード
"TIME & STYLE" Opening Announcement DM, Store Business Card

インテリア　Home Furnishings ｜ Japan

CL＋CD＋SB＝タイム アンド スタイル　TIME & STYLE
I＝永野敬子　Keiko Nagano

ダイレクトメール　Direct Mail

明かりに照らすと
ろうそくの炎がゆれるクリスマスカード

ささやかなライブのプレゼント告知が載ったインテリアショップの
クリスマスカード。カードを光に照らし揺らしてみるとイラストの
ろうそくの炎がゆれるようデザインされている。

A Christmas card with candle flames that flicker when the card is illuminated

A Christmas card for an interior shop that includes an announcement
of a small live present. The card is designed so that the flames on the
candles appear to flicker when the card is held up to the light and
moved backwards and forwards.

嬉しい喜びが伝わる新店舗案内DMと
集めて楽しいショップカード

DMはソファの型のカードの上にトレーシングペーパーに印刷した
イラストデザインをかぶせ、人が座っているように見せた。
ショップカードはそれぞれのショップイメージに合わせたソファの
型抜きで作成した。

A DM invitation for a new store that conveys a sense of joyous delight and store business cards that are a joy to collect

The DM consists of a card in the shape of a sofa with an illustrated
design printed on tissue paper placed over the top so that it looks like
someone is sitting on the sofa. The business cards were created using
die-cuts of different sofas to represent the different store images.

TIME AND STYLE at TOKYO MIDTOWN
GRAND OPEN
Fri 30th March 2007

TIME & STYLE EXISTENCE 4-27-15 Minamiaoyama Minato-ku Tokyo 107-0062 Phone 03-5464-5205 Fax 03-5464-5207

invitation

Opening Reception
Sun 25th March 2007
13:00–15:00
(Open 11:00–15:00)
at TIME & STYLE MIDTOWN

□ ささやかではありますが、オープニングパーティーを開催いたします。

TIME & STYLE
MIDTOWN

TIME & STYLE
FOREST

99

バー&ダイニング みつばち オープン案内DM
Bar & Dining Mitsubachi Opening Announcement DM

飲食店 Restaurant │ Japan

CL+DF+SB=オペレーションファクトリー Operation Factory
CD=南方 学 Manabu Minakata
AD+D=高井 聡 Satoshi Takai

A DM notifying of the opening of an eating establishment that conveys a "new kind of bar & dining experience"

A DM whose motif is the adult game of poker. On the back of each card is information about the establishment. One card can be removed and used as an invitation. Various printing processes have been combined to give an overall impression of quality.

〝Bar & Diningの新しい形〟を
伝える飲食店の開店案内DM

大人の遊びでもある〝ポーカー〟がモチーフのDM。
各カードの裏には店舗情報などを記載。1枚のみ
インビテーションカードとして使用できるように取り外せる。
様々な加工を施し、全体的にグレード感を出した。

バー&ダイニング Vano オープン案内DM
Bar & Dining Vano Opening Announcement DM

飲食店 Restaurant │ Japan

CL=JK コーポレーション JK corporation
CD=南方 学 Manabu Minakata
AD+D=高井 聡 Satoshi Takai
DF+SB=オペレーションファクトリー Operation Factory

表面と中面のギャップが
開封した際の〝驚き・感動〟を
与える飲食店DM

表面は黒を基調に紙の質感も高級感を持たせ、
中面は表面とのギャップを狙い、全面ゴールド仕様にして
ゴージャス感を出した。表面はタントセレクト、
中面はスペシャリティーズという全く異なった素材を合紙した。

An eating establishment DM whose back and inside convey a sense of "surprise and excitement" when opened

The front has black as the underlying tone and the quality of the paper impart a sense of luxuriousness, while the inside and back are entirely in gold for contrast and to give an impression of gorgeousness. Two completely different materials (Tant Select for the back and Specialties for the middle) were used together.

ヘアサロン クリスマスカード、パーティ案内状
Hair Salon Christmas Card, Party Invitation Card

美容院 Hair Salon｜Japan

CL＝k-two エフェクト k-two effect co., ltd.
AD＝芦谷正人 Masato Ashitani
D＝越智ゆみ Yumi Ochi
DF＋SB＝DRIVE , Inc.

はばたく〝蝶〟で
コンセプトを表現した
クリスマスカードと招待状

ステークスホルダー、メディア関係者向けの
クリスマスカードとパーティの案内状。
女性を美しくする業界として〝さなぎ〟から
〝蝶〟へのコンセプトにのっとり表現した。
箔押し加工のカバーとトムソン加工の蝶を使用。

A Christmas card and invitation that get across their message using an image of a "butterfly" emerging from a "chrysalis"

A Christmas card and invitation aimed at stakeholders and members of the media. Based on the fact that the client is involved in the business of making women beautiful, the concept of a "chrysalis" metamorphosing into a "butterfly" was chosen. Gold leaf was used on the cover while the butterfly is die-cut.

ABSOLUT ICEBAR TOKYO パーティ招待状
ABSOLUT ICEBAR TOKYO Party Invitation DM

飲料品メーカー　Beverage Manufacturer｜Japan

CL＝アブソルート・アイスバー東京　ABSOLUT ICEBAR TOKYO
CD＝浅尾浩一　Koichi Asao
AD＋D＝青井達也　Tatsuya Aoi
DF＋SB＝ノーザン グラフィックス　Northern Graphics

すべて氷でできたバーで
開かれたパーティの招待状

ABSOLUT ICEBAR TOKYO のインテリアリニューアルを
記念して開催されたパーティの招待状。
インテリアのテーマとリンクしたギミックが、ジグソーパズルや
ミラーボールで取り入れられている。
ホログラム紙を使用し、氷でできたバー空気感を表現。

An announcement and party
invitation for the first anniversary
of a bar made completely from ice

An announcement and party invitation for the first
anniversary of the Absolut Ice Bar Tokyo. The announcement
has a jigsaw puzzle motif, and the invitation a mirror ball
motif. Made using hologram paper, the products give a sense
of the atmosphere and disco-like flamboyance of the bar.

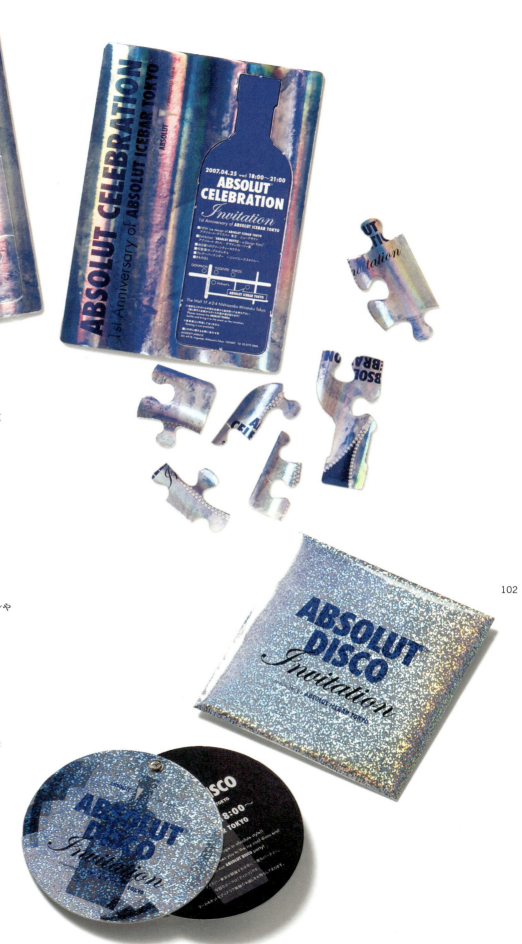

102

事務所移転案内DM
Office Relocation Announcement DM

デザイン会社 Design Firm | Japan

CL＋DF＋SB＝イネガデザイン　INEGA. D inc
AD＝渡部浩明　Hiroaki Watanabe
D＝渡辺真由子　Mayuko Watanabe

103

移転先の眺めの良さを
伝える引越しの案内状

新しい引越し先が30階という眺めの良い場所で
あったため、その眺めを見てもらいたいという考えから作成。
綺麗な夜景を表現するため、光沢PP加工し、
紙は厚手なものを選び、裏面の文字はシルバーの箔押しにした。

A moving announcement that allows
recipients to appreciate the wonderful
view from the new address

Created because the view from the new address on the 30th floor
was so good the sender wanted recipients to share it. In order to
capture the beautiful night view, thick cardboard with a glossy
finish was chosen and the lettering on the back put in silver leaf.

オープニングレセプション案内〝CELINE meets Mika NIgagawa〟〝ブギーマニアコレクション〟
Reception Opening Invitation Card "CELINE meets Mika NIgagawa" "Boogie Mania Collection"

CL＝セリーヌ CELINE
AD＋D＋SB＝グルーヴィジョンズ groovisions
P＝蜷川実花 Mika Ninagawa

アパレル Apparel｜Japan

ダイレクトメール Direct Mail

コレクションの特色を活かし ブランドのイメージを 伝える案内状

蜷川実花とのコラボレーションコレクションの
オープニングレセプション案内では、蜷川の鮮やかで
幻想的な色彩を活用。〝ブギーマニアコレクション〟
の案内では、ブランドの顔であるブギーバッグの形に
封筒を型抜きしてフィルムを貼り、新作バッグ同様
アニマルモチーフを使用したカードを見せた。

An invitation that conveys an image of a new collaborative collection

An invitation to the opening reception for a
collaborative collection with Mika Ninagawa features
the dreamy colors favored by Ninagawa, which are quite
different from the colors usually associated with the
brand. On the other hand, an invitation to the "Boogie
Mania Collection" includes an envelope cut out in the
shape of a bag with film attached on the inside so that
the card inside featuring the same new animal motif as
the bag is visible.

104

CL＝ワールド通商　World Commerce Corporation
AD＝美澤 修　Osamu Misawa
D＝梶谷聡美　Satomi Kajitani
SB＝美澤修デザイン室　Osamu Misawa Design Room Co., Ltd.

ダイレクトメール　Direct Mail

105

1年を通して使える時計ブランドの
カレンダー式新年の挨拶

フランク・ミュラーの 2008年カレンダー。
顧客向けに新年の挨拶として作成。
単なる年賀状ではなく、1年を通して使ってもらえるように、
全ページのデザインが異なる週めくりカレンダーとした。

A New Year greeting for a watch
brand that can be used as a
calender all year round

Franck Muller's 2008 calendar. Created as a New Year
greeting aimed at customers. Instead of a traditional New
Year card, the greeting takes the form of a page-a-week
calendar with each page featuring a different design,
something that can be used all year round.

ダイレクトメール　Direct Mail

美味しいコーヒーと こだわりのフードを楽しめる カフェの開店案内状

フードの写真がクリスマスツリーに飾る
オーナメントになっている。小さな手提げ袋にたくさんの
フードを詰め込み、店の魅力や楽しみを表現した。
各オーナメントの裏にそれぞれのこだわりを
文字で入れた。

An opening announcement for a cafe that offers good coffee and fine food

Photographs of the food available in the cafe double as
Christmas tree ornaments. Numerous food items are
crammed into a small shopping bag, enabling customers to
get a taste of what it feels like to shop inside. On the back
of each ornament is a note explaining what makes each
item special.

106

年賀状
New Year Greeting Card

個人 Private │ Japan

CL＋AD＋D＋SB＝吉田ユニ Yuni Yoshida
P＝米田 渉 Wataru Yoneda

変顔とビジュアルでハッピーな感じを表した年賀状

お世話になっている方々に送るための年賀状。
昔見た、『志村けんのだいじょぶだぁ』のような鏡を使った
変顔を思い出し、かっこよく表現できないかと考えたもの。
鏡は使用できなかったので、合成で作成。

A New Year card that expresses happy feelings through a funny face and visuals

A New Year card for sending to people who've been of
assistance during the year. The idea was to come up with a
funny face with glasses like those worn years ago by Japanese
comedian Ken Shimura in the TV show Daijobu da. Actual
glasses couldn't be used, so they were created artificially.

小岐須雅之個展 案内状
MASAYUKI OGISU Exhibition Invitation Card

個人 Private │ Japan

CL＝小岐須雅之 MASAYUKI OGISU
AD＋D＝青井達也 Tatsuya Aoi
DF＋SB＝ノーザン グラフィックス Northern Graphics

出来上がった絵とコンセプトから生まれた経典のような個展の案内状

独特の色使いと女性像で知られる小岐須雅之の
個展案内状。表面を合紙し存在感を出し、開けると中から
長い経典のようなじゃばら折りが出てくる仕掛けとなっている。
じゃばら折りは機械では折れないため手仕事で行った。

An exhibition invitation in the form of a sutra and based on the paintings and concept

An invitation to a solo exhibition by Masayuki Ogisu, noted
for his originality in his use of color and his depiction of
female figures. Laminated paper was used on the cover for
impact and the invitation was designed so that when opened a
long, pleated sheet of paper like a sutra popped out. Because
pleating can't be done with a machine, it was folded by hand.

ナノ・ユニバース東京 レセプションパーティDM
nano・universe TOKYO Reception Party Invitation DM

CL＝ナノ・ユニバース nano・universe
CD＋AD＋D＝NESCO
DF＋SB＝Nigrec Design

アパレル Apparel│Japan

ダイレクトメール　Direct Mail

開くとショップが飛び出す
セレクトショップの
レセプションパーティの案内状

セレクトショップの5周年記念のレセプションパーティの
案内状。カードの開閉は紐かけ式で、飛び出す絵本の要領で、
開くと擬似的にショップの形が再現される。

An invitation to a reception for a
boutique in which a shop pops up
when opened

An invitation to a reception marking the fifth anniversary of a
boutique. The card is the type that is opened and closed with a
ribbon and is based on the same principle as a pop-up picture
book, with the shape of the shop popping up when the
invitation is opened.

108

CL=鉄板焼 周　JYU Teppan-Yaki JYU
CD＋AD＋D=高井 聡　Satoshi Takai
DF＋SB=オペレーションファクトリー　Operation Factory

ダイレクトメール　Direct Mail

大人の女性向け、触れて伝わる インパクトと期待感を表現した 飲食店オープン案内DM

ターゲットにあわせ上質で高級感のあるデザインと素材を
選択。紋様部分をUVシルクニス厚盛りし、
さらに強調するために、他の箇所は凹型押しに。
想像以上の〝浮き出し〟により今までにないインパクトを生んだ。

A DM for an eating establishment aimed at adult females that conveys a sense of impact and anticipation in a palpable way

Refined, luxurious design and materials were chosen to match
the target audience. The patterned area was raised using
silk-screen UV varnish and further emphasized by recessing the
other areas. This "embossing" was more effective than
anticipated, producing an impact not seen up to now.

109

CL＝モーテル MOTEL INC.
CD＋AD＝NESCO
D＝OZAKI TSUYOSHI DESIGN
DF＋SB＝Nigrec Design

ダイレクトメール Direct Mail

航空会社とのコラボコレクションの旅や飛行機をテーマにした招待状

MOTELとルフトハンザとのコラボレーションコレクションの展示会DM。ネガフィルム、透け感を活かしたグラフィックや、窓枠を型ヌキした飛行機の形などを利用し、ブランドイメージである旅や飛行機を表現した。

An invitation to a collaboration with an airline company with a travel and airplane theme

An exhibition DM relating to a collaborative collection between MOTEL and Lufthansa. The brand image of travel and airplanes was expressed using graphics that made use of negative film and a see-through look as well as cutout windows in the shape of airplanes.

110

フジカラーネガシート

Shilhouette of Hair 案内DM
Shilhouette of Hair Announcement DM

美容院 Hair Salon ｜ Japan

CL＝ヘアースタジオビューティーヴィラ Hair Studio Beauty Villa
CD＝明富士治郎 Jiro Akefuji
AD＋D＝池澤 樹 Tatsuki Ikezawa
C＝中里智史 Satoshi Nakazato
SB＝東急エージェンシー Tokyu Agency Inc.

ダイレクトメール　Direct Mail

女性のカラーリングされた髪形を
アイデアのもとにした
美容室のDM

顧客に対して季節の変わり目の来店を促す美容室のDM。
女性3人のスタッフを3つのシルエットで表現した。
中のメッセージカードを差し替えると、
髪型に抜かれた穴から髪色が変わるように見える。

DM for a beauty salon
inspired by female hairstyles

DM for a beauty salon designed to encourage customers to
visit at the change of seasons. The three staff members are
represented by three silhouettes. When the message card
inside is switched, the color of the hair visible through the
hairstyle-shaped die-cut holes appears to change.

112

ハッピーバースデー〝Mia〟バースデーカード
Happy Birthday Mia Birthday Card

パッケージブランド Packaging Brand │ UK

CL＝SiebertHead Ltd
CD＋D＝Ben Cox
D＝Tim Farrer
DF＝SiebertHead Ltd
DF＋SB＝Studio 6.3

帝王切開で生まれた
赤ん坊のバースデーカードを
ユーモラスに表現

帝王切開で生まれた赤ん坊用のユーモア感覚あふれた
誕生祝いカード。カードには封筒を開けるための
メスが添えられており、受け取った人はメスを使って
封筒を開封し、まるで帝王切開のようにカードを取り出す。

A humorous card for celebrating
the birth of a baby born by
Caesarean section

A humorous card to celebrate the birth of a baby born by
Caesarean section. The card comes together with a scalpel
for opening the envelope. The recipient uses the scalpel to
open the envelope and retrieve the card almost as if they
were performing a Caesarean section.

事務所移転案内DM
Office Relocation Announcement DM

個人 Private │ Japan

CL＋DF＋SB＝カラー Color.inc
CD＋AD＋D＝シラスノリユキ Noriyuki Shirasu

〝荷物〟をモチーフにした
事務所の移転案内DM

〝引越し〟を、すぐにイメージしてもらうため、
〝荷物〟をモチーフとしたDMを作成。手に取った時の
存在感を出すために、コースター用紙に印刷した。
形状も〝箱〟の形にすることで、擬似的な存在感を出した。

An office-relocation announcement
with a "luggage" motif

A "luggage" motif was chosen for this DM to quickly evoke an
image of a "relocation." The notice was printed on coaster
paper to ensure it had a presence when held in the hand. An
effort was also made to simulate the presence of luggage by
making it in the shape of a "box."

ミナ ペルホネン新商品展示会告知DM
minä perhonen New Product Exhibition Anouncement DM

アパレル Apparel ｜ Japan

CL=ミナ ペルホネン　minä perhonen
CD＋I=皆川 明　Akira Minagawa
AD=田中竜介　Ryusuke Tanaka
D=関本明子　Akiko Sekimoto
Printing Director=落合 崇　Takashi Ochiai
SB=ドラフト　DRAFT Co., Ltd.

ダイレクトメール　Direct Mail

モノトーンの世界から
カラフルな世界に変化する
新商品展示会の告知DM

オリジナルのテキスタイルで知られるファッションブランドの
新商品展示会の告知DM。封筒の表情が、中身を取り出すことに
よってモノトーンの世界からカラフルな世界に紙芝居のように
変化する仕組みになっている。

DM advertising an exhibition of new products that metamorphoses from a monotone world into a colorful world

DM for an exhibition of new products produced by a fashion
brand famous for its original textiles. The DM is designed in
such a way that the look of the envelope changes like a series of
picture cards from a monotone world to a colorful world when
the contents are removed.

114

Yuming F.C クリスマスカード
Yuming F.C Christmas Card

プロダクション Production ｜ Japan

CL＝Yuming F.C
AD＋D＝御代田尚子 Naoko Miyoda
P＝堀内僚太郎 Ryotaro Horiuchi
Food Coordinator＝御代田聡子 Satoko Miyoda
Producer＝中岡美奈子 Minako Nakaoka
DF＋SB＝ドラフト DRAFT Co., Ltd.

アーティストの世界観、クリスマスの空気感を伝えるクリスマスカード

ファンクラブメンバーに贈る Yuming からのクリスマスカード。
Yuming の世界観を大事に、クリスマスの優しくあたたかな
室内風景を写真で表現。二つ折りのシンプルな加工を
使いながらピアノの立体感を再現させた。

A Christmas card that captures the worldview of an artist and the atmosphere of Christmas

A Christmas message from Yuming directed at members of
her fan club. The emphasis was on capturing the worldview
of the artist and the atmosphere of Christmas. The card
was produced using partial cut-outs and a single fold to
achieve an effect that's between flat and three-dimensional.

n°11コレクション告知DM
n°11 Collection Annousement DM

アパレル Apparel ｜ Japan

ダイレクトメール　Direct Mail

CL=ナンバー11 n°11
CD=嶋村公子 Kimiko Shimamura
SB=シマムラ トーキョー コーポレーション Shimamura Tokyo Corporation

116

ほんのりあたたかな気持ちにさせてくれる風船づかいのコレクション招待状

アパレルブランドの2007年秋冬コレクションの招待状。コレクションのイメージを綴ったディレクターのポエムをヴィジュアル化。ハートが静かに落ちてくる様子をイメージし、ハート、風船の持つ空気感で表現した。

An invitation to a collection using balloons that fills the recipient with a slightly warm feeling

An invitation to the fall / winter 2007 collection of an apparel brand. The invitation is a visualization of a poem by the director who came up with the image for the collection. It conveys a sense of an atmosphere full of hearts and balloons based on an image of hearts falling.

24 seasons 〝つづるけしき、こころつづく展〟案内DM
24 seasons "Depicting scenes close to the heart" Exhibition Annoucement DM

商業施設 Commercial Facility │ Japan

CL=スパイラル spiral
AD+D=青木康子 Yasuko Aoki
DF+SB=パンゲア PANGAEA Ltd.

切れ目のない季節の移ろい、二十四節気をモチーフにした展覧会の案内状

表として見ていたイメージが、案内状を広げると裏に回り、別のイメージが現れる。イメージが回転するときに起こる小さな風や動きで展覧会のテーマを表現。折りの伸び縮みを利用することで、型抜き部分が回転する。

An invitation to an exhibition with a motif of seamless nature in the form of Japan's "24 seasons"

The image that appears to be the front rotates to the back when the invitation is opened. The faint breeze and movement that occurs as the image revolves express the exhibition's theme. Folds and cutouts were used, with the expansion and contraction of the folds causing the cutout section to rotate.

モチーフの花をグラフィカルに表現して作家の世界観を伝えた展覧会DM

内側一面に花柄を敷き詰め、外から見るとその花が少し透けて見え、裏面からは一部の花がこぼれ出ている。一見、白い世界だが、内側には花が溢れんばかりに詰まっているという表現で、作品のもつ華やかさを伝えた。

An exhibition DM that conveys a sense of the artist's worldview by expressing colorfully a flower motif

The inside of the DM is covered in a floral pattern and the whole designed so that when viewed from the outside the flowers are slightly visible and when viewed from the back some of them appear to be spilling out. A sense of the gorgeousness of the artist's work was conveyed by presenting a world that at first sight appears white but whose inside is crammed with flowers almost to the point of overflowing.

個展 ECHOS - INFINITY DM
ECHOS - INFINITY Exhibition Annoucement DM

ギャラリー Garelly │ Japan

CL=資生堂ギャラリー Shiseido Gallery
AD+D=青木康子 Yasuko Aoki
DF=パンゲア PANGAEA Ltd.

CL＋AD＋D＝佐野研二郎　Kenjiro Sano
D＋P＝岡本和樹　Kazuki Okamoto
SB＝MR_DESIGN

ダイレクトメール Direct Mail

118

受け取ったときの楽しさも
デザインした酉年の焼き鳥型
年賀状

焼き鳥が郵便受けに入っていたら楽しいという発想から生まれた
酉年の年賀状。リアルな焼き鳥の画像をカットアウトし、
郵便受けに入っていたときに驚く状況も同時にデザインした。

A yakitori-shaped New Year's greeting card
for the year of Rooster designed with the
circumstances of its reception in mind

A New Year's greeting card for the year of the Rooster whose concept was
based on the delight of finding some yakitori in one's mailbox. The card
was made by cutting out a realistic image of some yakitori, with the
design also taking into account the surprise the recipient would
experience when discovering it in their mailbox.

CL＝宣伝会議　Sendenkaigi
AD＋D＝鎌田順也　Junya Kamada
CW＝清松俊也　Toshiya Kiyomatsu
CW＝宇部信也　Shinya Ube
DF＋SB＝レバン　LEVAN inc.

講座を虫メガネに例え〝見つける〟ことの楽しさを表現した受講生募集DM

アートディレクター養成講座の受講生募集DM。
〝この講座は新しい自分を発見したり、新しい価値観を得る場〟
講座を虫メガネに例えて〝見つける〟ことの楽しさ、新鮮さを表現した。

A DM aimed at prospective students that conveys the joy of "discovery" by using a magnifying glass as a metaphor for the course

A DM seeking students for a course for training art directors. The course is an opportunity for students to discover a different side to themselves and obtain a new sense of values. This is conveyed through this offbeat DM. A magnifying glass is used as a metaphor for the course and represents the joy and freshness of "discovery."

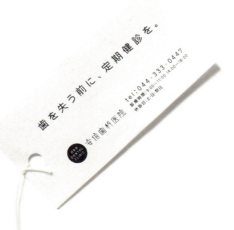

歯を失う前に、定期健診を。

tel:044-333-0447

安倍歯科医院

歯科医院DM
Dental Clinic DM

歯科 Dental Clinic｜Japan

CL＝安倍歯科医院　ABE DENTAL CLINIC
CD＋C＝矢谷 暁　Akira Yatani
AD＋D＝池澤 樹　Tatsuki Ikezawa
SB＝東急エージェンシー　Tokyu Agency Inc.

安倍歯科医院

封筒の中に
本物そっくりの歯が入った
歯科検診の呼びかけDM

歯科医院からの定期検診の呼びかけ。封筒の中には
歯を失う怖さを想起させる本物そっくりの歯とコピーの入った
タグが入っている。歯の模型は実際に患者の歯をつくる
歯科技工士が歯科用で使う素材で製作した。

A mail out promoting dental examinations consisting of an envelope containing a realistic mockup of some teeth

A mail out from a dental clinic promoting regular dental examinations. Inside the envelope is a tag containing a realistic copy of some teeth designed to remind people of the danger of losing one's teeth. The teeth are made from the same material actually used by the dental technicians who make patients' teeth.

Fat Lady 商品案内 DM
Fat Lady Product Announcement DM

化粧品メーカー Cosmetic Manufacturer │ Japan

CL=エナス ENAS Co., Ltd.
CD+AD=橋本孝久 Takahisa Hashimoto
CW=富永広紀 Hironori Tominaga
P=伊藤彰浩 Akihiro Ito
SB=デビッド・コミュニケーションズ David Communications

121

セルライト除去の高い効果を ヴィジュアルで伝える プロモーションDM

ボディラインが変形する女性をモチーフとし、製品の効果を
分かりやすく伝えた。コピーも「ボディラインは、変えられる。」から、
開くと「ボディラインは、これくらいかんたんに変えられる。」となる。

A promotional DM that communicates visually the effectiveness of a product in getting rid of cellulite

Simply communicate the benefit of the product using woman's motif
paper cut-out. The copy say "Your figure can be changed", once you
open the card, "See how easy you can change your figure."

〝ヘルプ〟募金カード
"Help" Donation Card

福祉 welfare work ｜ Germany

CL＝KINDERNOTHILFE E.V.
CD＝Matthias Schmidt
AD＝Martin Dlugosch
CW＝Dennis Lueck
SB＝Scholz & Friends

自分の寄付がどのような影響を与えるのかを視覚化した寄付金募集カード

ドイツ主要都市で宅送されたストリートチルドレンへの寄付を募るカード。送金用紙を引き抜くと、路上で寝ていた子どもが安全な家の中のベッドへと移る。寄付がどのような結果を生むのか視覚化した。

A card soliciting charitable donations that shows what effect a donation has

A card soliciting donations for street children delivered to homes in a major city in Germany. When the remittance form is pulled out, the child who was sleeping on the street moves to a bed in a safe home. This visualizes for recipients the results of their donations.

カーボンカード
Carbon Card

非営利団体 Non-profit Organization ｜ Malaysia

CL＝Woman's Aid Organisation (WAO)
CD＋AD＋CW＝Tan Kien Eng
AD＝Theresa Tsang
CW＝Valerie Chen
P＝Allen Dang
P＝Jesse Choo
SB＝Arc Worldwide Malaysia

日常的なカーボンと封筒を使用して 女性虐待の問題意識を高めた キャンペーン

開封前に誰かにいった今まで一番ひどい言葉を書くよう指示。
封筒をあけると、女性の顔にその言葉が傷跡を残している。
肉体的なものだけでなく、精神的な虐待がどれだけ犠牲者を
傷つけるか問題意識を高めさせた。

A campaign designed to raise awareness of female abuse that uses ordinary carbon paper and an envelope

Before opening the envelope one is asked to write down the
worst thing one has said to anyone. On opening the envelope,
these words appear on the face of a woman in the form of a scar.
The aim is to raise awareness of the damage inflicted on victims
not only by physical abuse, but also by mental cruelty.

イラストレーター名刺
Business Card of Illustlator

個人 Private｜Japan

CL＝伊藤明子 AKIKO ITO
AD＋D＝鎌田順也 Junya Kamada
DF＋SB＝レバン LEVAN inc.

絵の具チューブ型の
イラストレーターの名刺

イラスト→絵の具という分かりやすさをもとに人の
印象を色（空色）で表現した。デザインは控えめに、
イラストレーターの名前がさわやかに印象に残るようにした。

An illustrator's business card in
the shape of a tube of azure paint

Gives an impression of the owner using a color (azure)
based on the simplicity of the connection between
illustrations and paint. The design is low-key with the
emphasis on leaving a clear impression of the
illustrator's name in the mind of the recipient.

124

Amon's Delicious Catering ショップカード
Amon's Delicious Catering Shop Business Card

ケータリング Catering │ Austria

CL＝Wilhelm Amon Junior ＆ R 12
CD＝Cordula Alessandri
AD＋D＋I＝Stephan Kirsch
Text＝Cosima Reif
Text＝Felix Fenz
Text＝Gert Winkler
Production＝Reprozwoelf
DF＋SB＝alessandri design

多種多様なカッティングでおいしい料理の ケータリングとイベントプロデュースをする 会社を宣伝したショップカード

クライアントを、おいしい料理を作るだけでなく、
イベント全体の手配もするケータリング業界の何でも屋と
位置づけた。六臂のシヴァ神を彷彿させる古典的なスタイルの
イメージを意図的に使用し、会社の歴史を強調。

A shop card that uses different cuttings to inform event participants of issues

The client was positioned not only as a company that creates wonderful food, but also as a jack-of-all-trades within the catering industry able to arrange every aspect of an event. The history of the company was emphasized by intentionally using images with a classical style that resemble the six-armed Hindu god Shiva.

離婚弁護士 名刺
Divorce Lawyer Business Card

弁護士事務所 Legal Service │ Canada

CL＝James Mahon, LL. B.
CD＝Stephen Jurisic
CD＝Angus Tucker
AD＝Nellie Kim
CW＝Chris Hirsch
SB＝john st. advertising

名刺
Business Card

126

〝離婚〟をヴィジュアル化したユニークな
離婚専門弁護士用ビジネスカード

効果的でユニークな離婚専門弁護士用のビジネスカード。
限られたスペースで要点をシンプルに伝えるため、
名刺の真ん中にミシン目を入れ、分割可能にし、
誰にでもわかるように〝離婚〟をヴィジュアル化した。

A unique business card for a
divorce lawyer in which divorce is
given visual expression

A unique and effective business card for a divorce lawyer. In order to get the
message across simply using the limited space available, "divorce" is given visual
expression in a way likely to be understand by anyone by incorporating a
perforation down the middle of the card so that it can be divided in two.

WILLL 名刺
WILLL Business Card

個人 Private｜Austria

CL＝WILLL - Manufacturer, Archtecturer, Möbelkultur
CD＝Edi Keck
AD＝Cordula Alessandri
D＝Hans Proschofsky
DF＝Haslinger, Keck Wien
DF＋SB＝alessandri design

127

透明な封筒からその職業を象徴する
素材が透けてみえるビジネスカード

大きな木工所を営む父と、一人は建築家、もう一人は
インテリアショールームを営む息子たちに共通のデザインを
使用したビジネスカード。セロファンの封筒に文字を印刷し、
中にはベニア板や布などが入っている。

Business cards that offer a glimpse through
a transparent envelope of material that
symbolizes the industry of the holder

Business cards for a father who runs a large woodworking plant and his two sons,
one of whom is an architect and the other of whom runs an interior showroom,
which share the same design. The words are printed on a cellophane envelope,
inside of which are small sheets of veneer, fabric, and such like.

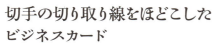

Anonima Francobolli 名刺
Anonima Francobolli Business Card

スタンプディーラー Stamp Dealing | Italy

CL＝Anonima Francobolli
CD＋AD＝Mauro Pastore
CD＋AD＝Masa Magnoni
CD＋AD＝Alessandro Floridia
D＋P＋I＝Paolo Sala
DF＋SB＝Cacao Design

名刺
Business Card

切手の切り取り線をほどこした
ビジネスカード

スタンプディーラーとしてイタリアを代表するクライアントの
ビジネスカード。切り取り線は切手のシートに
使用されているものとまったく同じ。
カードの端は銀箔加工してあり、特別な高級感を与えている。

A business card with perforations just like those on a stamp

A business card for a client that's a major player in the Italian stamp collecting and resale industry. The perforations are exactly the same as those that appear on sheets of stamps. The edges of the card are coated in silver leaf, giving it an air of luxuriousness.

Micromega 名刺
Micromega Business Card

映画 Cinema | Italy

CL＝Micromega
CD＋AD＝Mauro Pastore
CD＋AD＝Masa Magnoni
CD＋AD＝Alessandro Floridia
D＋P＋I＝Paolo Sala
DF＋SB＝Cacao Design

企業の良質さを伝える
映画プロダクションの
ビジネスカード

パリを拠点とした映画プロダクションのビジネスカード。
映写機に似たシンボルは、マルセル・デュシャンの作品を
参考にしている。ビジネスカードは、
ロゴまわりが切り抜いてあり、しおりとしても機能する。

A business card for a movie production company designed to evoke an image of high quality

A business card for a movie production company based in Paris. The logo, which resembles a movie projector, references an original work by Marcel Duchamp. The area around the logo is cut out, allowing the card to be used as a bookmark.

SHOP TOOL
ショップツール

PRODUCT
プロダクト

BOOK
書籍

ラフォーレ原宿 新年福袋
LAFORET HARAJUKU New Year Shopping Bag

商業施設 Commercial Facility｜Japan

CL＝ラフォーレ原宿 LAFORET HARAJUKU Co., Ltd.
AD＋SB＝野田凪 Nagi Noda
P＝内田将二 Shoji Uchida
Stylist＝枝光理絵 Rie Edamitsu
Hair Make＝小西神紳士 Shinji Komishikami

ショップツール　Shop Tool

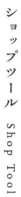

131

購入後の女性を
キュートに見せる着せかえ型の福袋

ラフォーレ原宿の新年福袋。ショートパンツや
ミニスカートを履いた女性の腰の部分の写真を使用し、
女性が腕にかけて持つと、ちょうど腰の部分にバッグが
重なり可愛く見えるという仕掛けになっている。

A grab bag designed to make the
purchaser look cute

A New Year's grab bag from Laforet Harajuku. The bags used
photographs of the hip region of women wearing short pants or
miniskirts and was designed in such a way that when women
hung it over their arm the image on the bag was superimposed
over their own hip region, making them look cute.

CL＝竹尾　TAKEO Co., Ltd.
AD＝水野 学　Manabu Mizuno
D＝古屋貴広　Takahiro Furuya
D＝仲山慎哉　Shinya Nakayama
DF＝グッドデザインカンパニー　good design company
SB＝グッドデザインカンパニー　good design company Co., Ltd.

ショップツール　Shop Tool

132

高級霜降り肉の塊に見える
ショッピングバッグ

高級黒毛和牛を使用したすき焼・しゃぶしゃぶで
知られる老舗〝浅草今半〟を仮想の
クライアントとして展示会で発表された。
鮮やかな肉色に綺麗にさしが入った
霜降り肉の塊がそのまま紙袋になっている。

A shopping bag that looks like a chunk of high-grade marbled beef

Displayed at an exhibition with Asakusa Imahan, a
restaurant famous for its sukiyaki and shabu-shabu
made using kuroge wagyu beef, as the hypothetical
client. The bag resembles a chunk of marbled beef with
the string passing neatly through the bright flesh color.

ベトナムレストラン メニュー
Vietnam Restaurant Menu
飲食店　Restaurant ｜ Japan

CL＝キッチン　kitchen
AD＋D＝田中竜介　Ryusuke Tanaka
SB＝ドラフト　DRAFT Co., Ltd.

現地で使われている笠を使用した
ベトナムレストランのメニュー

ベトナムで実際にかぶられている笠を使用して、
その形に合わせてレイアウトされたメニュー。
本物のベトナムのアイテムを手に取りながら食事のメニューを
考えることによって、料理をより楽しむことができる。

A menu for a Vietnamese restaurant that employs a conical straw hat like those worn in Vietnam

A menu that uses a conical straw hat like those actually worn in
Vietnam and is laid out following the shape of the hat. Because
patrons can handle a part of the real Vietnam as they consider
the menu, they can get more enjoyment out of the meal.

EVANCE ショッピングバッグ
EVANCE Shopping Bag

時計販売 Watch Sales | Japan

CL=エバンス　EVANCE INC.
CD=田島康寛　Yasuhiro Tajima
AD+D=柳田昌信　Akinobu Yanagida
P=平田浩基　Hiromoto Hirata
DF+SB=マック東京　MAQ inc. TOKYO

ショップツール　Shop Tool

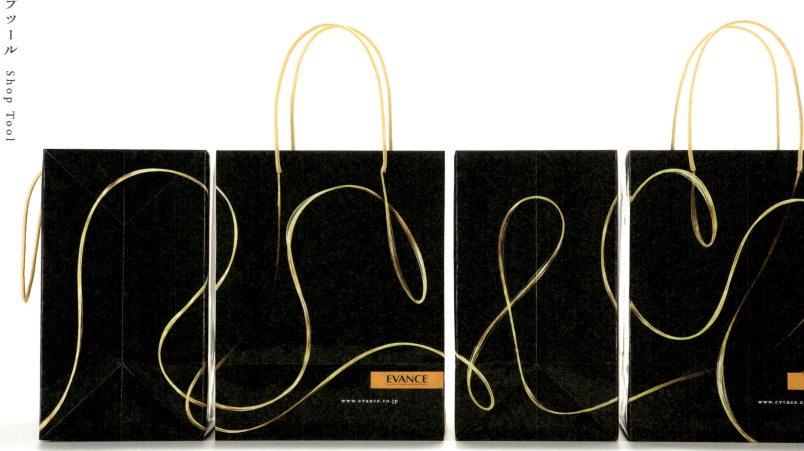

シックな中にも遊び心のある
ブランドイメージを伝える
ショッピングバッグ

持ち手から連なる紐のデザインで永遠に続く時間を
表現した高級時計店のペーパーバッグ。女性が肩からかけても
持ち歩けるよう紐の長さに配慮。光の表現及び背景を写真にし、
時間というものの存在感を引き出した。

A shopping bag that conveys a brand image that is chic yet playful

A paper bag for a luxury watch store that represents never-ending time with a design featuring ribbons running from the handles. Careful thought was given to the length of the ribbons so that women would feel comfortable walking around with the bag over their shoulder. The presence of time was brought out by using photographs to depict the colors and background on the bag.

美容院ショッピングバッグ
Hair Salon Shopping Bag

美容院 Hair Salon ｜ Japan

CL＝ミューズ muse
CD＋AD＋D＝永松りょうこ Ryoko Nagamatsu
SB＝東急エージェンシー Tokyu Agency Inc.

エクステのお下げ髪が
持ち手になったペーパーバッグ

エクステンションが持ち手になっているペーパーバッグ。
カラーサンプリングを兼ね、自由なスタイルを提案する
美容院として髪の毛という素材そのものの魅力を活かし、
変わったものを作り上げた。

Paper bags in which pigtail
extensions serve as handles

These paper bags have handles that are actually hair
extensions. They double as color samples, and were created
as something a bit different that makes the most of the
natural appeal of hair as a material for a beauty salon that
promotes carefree styles.

135

ジュエリーブランド ショッピングバッグ
Jewelry Brand Shopping Bag

ジュエリーブランド Jewelry Brand ｜ Japan

CL＋SB＝イー・エム・デザイン e.m. design Co., Ltd.
CD＝飛田眞義 Masayoshi Tobita
D＝大森智哉 Tomoya Omori

目立たず目立つ、
縦と横の2つの持ち手がある
ショッピングバッグ

ロゴも持ち手も横向きだが、縦にも持てるよう持ち手がついた
ショッピングバッグ。客に商品以外で驚きと楽しみを
プレゼントするため、えっと驚くデザインではあるけれど、
派手にはせず、目を惹くデザインを採用した。

A shopping bag with two handles
attached vertically and horizontally
that's striking without being showy

A shopping bag on which both the logo and handle are
horizontal but with an additional handle that also enables it
to be carried vertically. A startling item that uses an
eye-catching design to provide customers with something
other than a product that promises to surprise and delight
without being too showy.

Stopin Grow ショッピングバッグ
Stopin Grow Shopping Bag

製薬 Pharmaceuticals | Germany

CL＝The Mentholatum Company Ltd.
CD＝Burkhard von Scheven
CD＋AD＝David Mously
CD＋CW＝Jan Harbeck
P＝Michael Terry
Account＝Henning Gutmann
Account＝Christian Krah
SB＝Jung von Matt AG

ショップツール Shop Tool

持ってもらうことで見る人に
爪噛み癖を意識させる
プラスティックバッグ

爪に塗り、強烈な苦味で噛むのを止めさせると同時に、
爪の成長を促進する製品の広告。歯を見せ開いた口が
プラスティックバッグの持ち手の部分になっており、
手を入れれば、まるで爪を噛んでいるかのように見える。

A plastic bag that draws attention to nail-biting when carried around

An advertisement for a product that is applied to nails that
promotes the growth of nails and whose strongly bitter taste also
prevents nail-biting. The handle part of the bag resembles an
open mouth with the teeth bared so that when someone puts
their hand through it looks like their nails are being bitten.

Nail biter?
stop'n grow helps.

136

コレクション内祝い袋
Family gift bag for the brand's debut collection

アパレル　Apparel │ Japan

CL＋SB＝メルシーボークー、mercibeaucoup,
CD＝宇津木えり Eri Utsgi
D＝井上庸子 Yoko Inoue

めでたさ、日本人らしさをもとにした レジ袋素材の内祝い袋

宇津木えりのブランドのデビューコレクションの来訪者に
感謝の気持ちを伝えるために作成。日本風だが、重々しくなく、
カジュアルでチープ感があるように仕上げるため、
レジ袋の素材を用いた。当日はアンパンを入れて配布。

A "family celebration" bag made from store bag material that expresses auspiciousness and a quintessentially Japanese flavor

Created to convey a sense of gratitude towards visitors to the
brand's debut collection. To make it quintessentially Japanese
yet at the same time casual and neither expensive-looking nor
solemn, store bag material was used. On the day the bags were
distributed with bean-jam buns inside them.

Nu-Cube フュージョンレストラン ツール
Nu-Cube Fusion Restaurant Tools

飲食店 Restaurant │ Italy

CL＝Nu- Cube Fusion Restaurant
CD＋AD＝Mauro Pastore
CD＋AD＝Masa Magnoni
CD＋AD＝Alessandro Floridia
D＋P＋I＝Giulia Landini
DF＋SB＝Cacao Design
Interior Design Project＝Arch. Nisi Magnoni

フュージョン・レストランの ショップカードとメニュー

女性の感性が活かされたミランにある
フュージョン・レストランのショップカードとメニュー。
花や竹など自然の要素を用いて、優雅で繊細で
ぜいたくなアジアンテイストを表現した。
ショップカードは箸置きになる。

Fusion restaurant business card and menu

A business card and menu with a feminine touch for
a fusion restaurant in Milan. Both use natural
elements such as flowers and bamboo to express an
elegant, delicate, luxurious Asian taste.
The business card doubles as a chopstick rest.

もったいないカレンダー
Waste Me Not Calendar 'Mottainai'

広告代理店 Advertising Agency │ Japan

CL+SB=読売広告社 YOMIKO ADVERTISING INC.
CD+CW=藤崎 実 Minoru Fujisaki
AD=永瀬裕司 Yuji Nagase
D=遠藤輪香子 Wakako Endo
P=伊藤之一 Yukikazu Ito
I=大菅雅晴 Masaharu Ohsuga

Producer=中山喜芳 Kiyoshi Nakayama
Printing Director=穴沢幸夫 Yukio Anazawa
Food Coordinaoter=福岡裕子 Hiroko Fukuoka
Naming=Noriko & Don Carrol
Assistant=たなべむつみ Mutsumi Tanabe

プロダクト Product

138

使用後は裏面を
メモ用紙として使える
今までにないカレンダー

モノを大切にする精神の啓蒙をしようと考え、
世代や年齢、国境を越えて、誰にでも関係が持てる
カレンダーに着目。ビジュアル、記載、紙の素材、使い方、
すべてを〝もう一度使おう〟というコンセプトで貫いた。

A unique calendar whose pages can be turned over and used as memo paper after use

In an effort to highlight the importance of respecting things, the idea came about to focus on calendars, which everyone can relate to regardless of their generation, age, or nationality. The concept of 'reuse' is common throughout the entire calendar, from the overall look and entries to the paper and the way the calendar is used.

ORIGAMI みどりいろ／そらいろ
ORIGAMI green color/blue color

和紙制作 Japanese Paper Manufacturer｜Japan

CL＝Pd Ltd.／紙舘島勇 Pd Ltd. / Kamiyakata Shimayu Ltd.
AD＋P＝加藤建吾 Kengo Kato
D＝山田靖子 Yasuko Yamada
D＝竹中智博 Tomohiro Takenaka
D＝新井 崇 Takashi Arai
D＝草野 剛 Tsuyoshi Kusano
P＝宮本敬文 Keibun Miyamoto
PR＝三ツ橋憲司 Kenji Mitsuhashi
DF＋SB＝タグボート2 TUGBOAT2
Artwork＝山崎夏菜 Kana Yamazaki (paper art)
PR Manager＝小川 弾 Dan Ogawa

プロダクト Product

〝本来の色〟を伝えるために
〝写真〟をモチーフとした
今までにない折り紙

色というものは、本来世の中のあらゆるものが持つ
〝色〟が源である。世の中の人すべて、特に子どもに、
〝本来の色〟というものを伝えるため、今までにない〝写真〟を
モチーフにした折り紙を制作した。

Origami paper with a hitherto
unseen "photograph" motif designed
to promote "original colors"

Colors originated in the 'colors' of all the various things that
exist in the world. This origami paper was produced with a
hitherto unseen 'photograph' motif designed to promote these
'original colors' to everyone in the world, particularly children.

TONE 2008 触覚性カレンダー
TONE 2008 tactile Calendar

デザイン会社 Design Firm | Switzerland

CL＝TONE / CAMPICHE / PRO GRAVUR
CD＋AD＋D＋I＝Sonia Biétry
P＝Stéphane Dondicol
Embossing Engraver＝Pro Gravur
DF＋SB＝TONE

プロダクト　Product

視覚障害者と健常者の境界線を取り払うカレンダー

1つの製品のなかに、目が不自由な人のためには点字とエンボス、
視力が落ち始めている人のためには大きく、コントラストが強い数字、
視力に問題がない人のためには色彩と細かいヴィジュアルを採用した。

A calendar that does away with the distinction between people with and without visual impairments

This single product employs Braille and embossed lettering for the blind;
large, high contrast lettering for those whose eyesight is starting to weaken;
and colorful, detailed visuals for those with no eyesight problems.

Now Wash Your Hands カレンダー
Now Wash Your Hands Calendar

トイレ個室製造メーカー　Toilet Cubicle Manufacturer │ UK

CL＝Patrick Wilson (Thrislington Cubicles)
CD＝Greg Quinton
D＝Tony St De Croix
D＝Steve Owen
Printing＝Presstige Print
SB＝The Partners

1年分の石鹸でできた 〝さぁ、手を洗って〟カレンダー

トイレ個室製造メーカーが作成した限定版コレクター
アイテムのカレンダー。毎日切り取って使うことができる
1年分365個の実際の石鹸が吊るされカレンダーの形に
なっている。試作には4ヶ月を要した。

A "don't forget to wash your hands" calendar consisting of a year's worth of soap

A limited edition collectors' calendar produced by a toilet cubicle manufacturer. The calendar is in the form of 365 actual cakes of hanging soap,
one of which can be removed and used for each day of the year. Four
months were spent making the calendar.

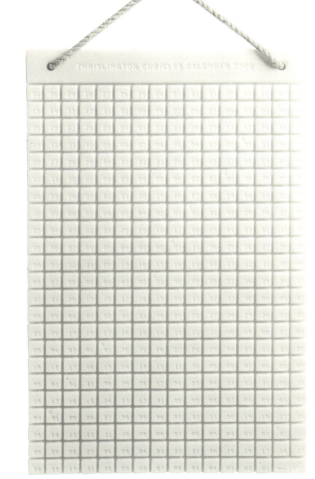

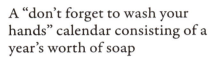

Spend a Penny カレンダー
Spend a Penny Calendar

トイレ個室製造メーカー　Toilet Cubicle Manufacturer │ UK

CL＝Patrick Wilson (Thrislington Cubicles)
CD＝Aziz Cami
D＝Greg Quinton
Printing＝Presstige Print
DF＋SB＝The Partners

ペニー硬貨を移動させてゆく 〝spend a penny〟カレンダー

365個のペニー大の溝があり、コインを毎日挿入し移動させていく
カレンダー。昔、トイレに入るには1旧ペニーを1枚挿入しなければ
ならなかったことから、〝spend a penny〟とは〝トイレに行く〟の意。

"Spend a penny" calendar that shifts coins around

A calendar with 365 penny-sized slots that
shifts coins that are fed into it each day. To
"spend a penny" means to go to the
bathroom, since a long time ago one had to
insert an old penny coin in coin-operated
locks on public lavatories.

東京ガス カレンダー、プレミアムブック
Tokyo Gas Calender, Premium Book

エネルギー Enegy｜Japan

CL＝東京ガス TOKYO GAS Co., Ltd.
AD＝安西葉子 Yoko Yasunishi
D＝林裕輔 Yusuke Hayashi
SB＝ドリルデザイン DRILL DESIGN CO., LTD.

プロダクト　Product

ガスの魅力を伝える
ガスコンロのゴトク型カレンダー

家庭向けに改めてガスの魅力を伝えるために作られた
ガスコンロの〝ゴトク〟型のカレンダー。
郵送を前提に、紙のプラモデルのように組み立てられる形にし、
ボール紙を三重にして持ったときのパーツ感を出した。

A calendar in the shape of a gas stove trivet that emphasizes the appeal of gas

A calendar in the shape of a gas stove trivet designed to remind
households of the appeal of gas. With mailing in mind, it was
made of cardboard in separate parts that can be assembled like
a plastic model. Three layers of cardboard were used so that
when picked up the finished product feels like the real thing.

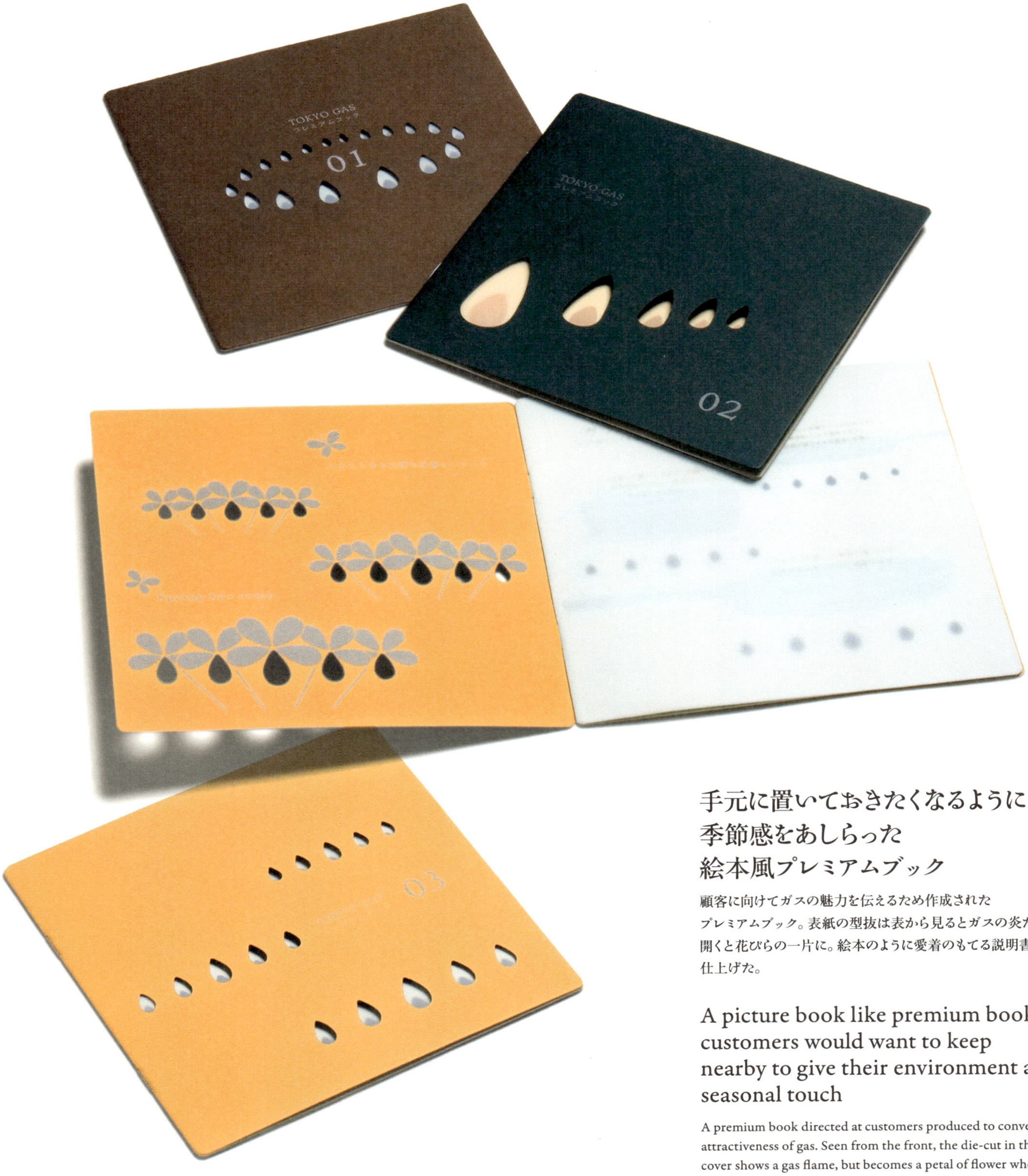

143

手元に置いておきたくなるように
季節感をあしらった
絵本風プレミアムブック

顧客に向けてガスの魅力を伝えるため作成された
プレミアムブック。表紙の型抜は表から見るとガスの炎だが、
開くと花びらの一片に。絵本のように愛着のもてる説明書に
仕上げた。

A picture book like premium book customers would want to keep nearby to give their environment a seasonal touch

A premium book directed at customers produced to convey the attractiveness of gas. Seen from the front, the die-cut in the cover shows a gas flame, but becomes a petal of flower when the book is opened. The book was designed to be a manual that users would form an attachment to, much like a picture book.

ブックカバー
Book Cover

書店 Bookstore｜Japan

CL＝白光堂書店　Hakkodo Book Store
AD＋D＝鎌田順也　Junya Kamada
CW＝清松俊也　Toshiya Kiyomatsu
DF＋SB＝レバン　LEVAN inc.

プロダクト　Product

144

店のアイデンティティを表現し、
なおかつ広告として機能する
ブックカバー

スピード感のあるコミュニケーションを目指し、
本が読まれる状況を想像させることを意図した。
オーソドックスな印刷でコストを下げ、シンプルな
デザインでコミュニケーションスピードを大切にした。

Book covers that express the
identity of a store and also function
as advertisements

Designed as a speedy form of communication that
encourages people to envision circumstances in which books
are read. Costs were kept to a minimum by using orthodox
printing methods and a high value set on communication
speed by employing simple design.

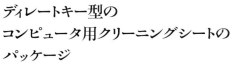

'delete' コンピュータークリーニング用シート
'delete' Computer Cleaning Wipes

パッケージブランド Packaging Brand │ UK

CL＝Reckitt and Benckiser
CD＝Noma Bar
D＝Ben Cox
DF＝SiebertHead Ltd
DF＋SB＝Studio 6.3

ディレートキー型の
コンピュータ用クリーニングシートの
パッケージ

コンピュータ・キーボードの delete〝削除〟キーの
見かけを模したコンピュータ用クリーニングシート。
パソコンの汚れを落とすことのアナロジーとなっている。
生分解性プラスチックを真空成形加工した。

A package for a computer cleaning
sheet in the shape of a delete key

A package for a computer cleaning sheet whose appearance
resembles the delete key on a computer keyboard. The
analogy is that of getting rid of the dirt on a computer. The
package is made of vacuum formed biodegradable plastic.

プロダクト Product

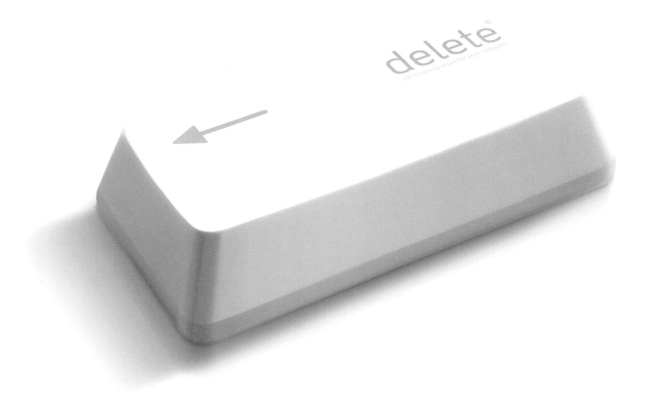

Muji ライトバルブ パッケージ
Muji Light Bulb Packaging

日用品メーカー Commodity Manufacturer | UK

CL＝Muji
CD＝Noma Bar
CD＝Amy Lupton
DF＝SiebertHead Ltd
DF＋SB＝Studio 6.3

プロダクト Product

3つの用途をもつ
電球のシンプルなパッケージ

無印良品が日常生活用品に活かしている
実用的なアプローチを採用したシンプルな電球のパッケージ。
はじめはパッケージとして、次にランプシェードとして、
最後には電球を廃棄する際の箱として利用できる。

Simple packaging for a
lightbulb that has three
different uses

Simple packaging for a lightbulb based on the practical
approach Muji adopts for its household goods. First it's used
as packaging, then it can be used as a lampshade, and finally
it can be used as a container when disposing of the lightbulb.

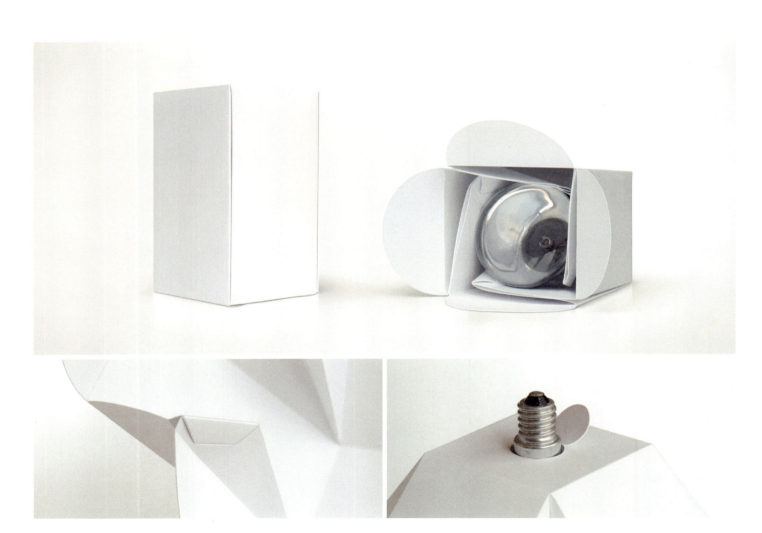

146

Global Warming マグカップ
Global Warming Mugs

パッケージブランド Packaging Brand｜UK

CL＝The House
CD＋D＋I＝Ben Cox
DF＋SB＝Studio 6.3

エネルギーの無駄遣いが
環境に与える影響について
考えさせられるマグカップ

気候の変化に対する関心を高めるために
デザインされたマグカップ。
温度変化で色が変わるインクを使用することで、
雪だるまの絵柄が変化し、ひとたびお湯が注がれると
雪だるまは溶けてしまう。

A mug designed to raise
awareness of the impact on the
environment of wasting energy

A mug designed to promote greater interest in climate
change. The mug is made using ink that changes color as
the temperature changes causing the snowman design
on the mug to appear to temporarily melt whenever hot
water is poured into the mug.

"Bear Do" ファイル DE バッグ
"Bear Do" File DE Bag

航空会社 Airline｜Japan

CL＝北海道国際航空　Hokkaido International Airlines
SB＝マルモ印刷　Marumo Printing Co., Ltd.

〝もったいない〟精神を貫いた
クリアファイルとして
再使用できるバッグ

資料が入れて送られてきた封筒を捨てるのはもったいない
という発想から生まれた、切り取るとクリアファイル
になるバッグ。切り取り後の廃棄部分は全体の20%。
素材もリサイクル性が高いものを利用している。

A reusable envelope and bag full
of the "mottainai" spirit

An envelope and bag, part of which can be torn off and
reused as a clear file, based on the idea that throwing away
envelopes mailed with documents inside them is
mottainai, or wasteful. Tearing off the reusable section
leaves 20% of the original envelope remaining in the form
of waste. An emphasis was also placed on using recyclable
materials.

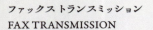

ファックス トランスミッション
FAX TRANSMISSION

製紙メーカー Paper Manufacturer ｜ Japan

CL＝竹尾　Takeo Co., Ltd.
AD＋D＝平林奈緒美　Naomi Hirabayashi
SB＝プラグイングラフィック　PLUG - IN GRAPHIC

プロダクト　Product

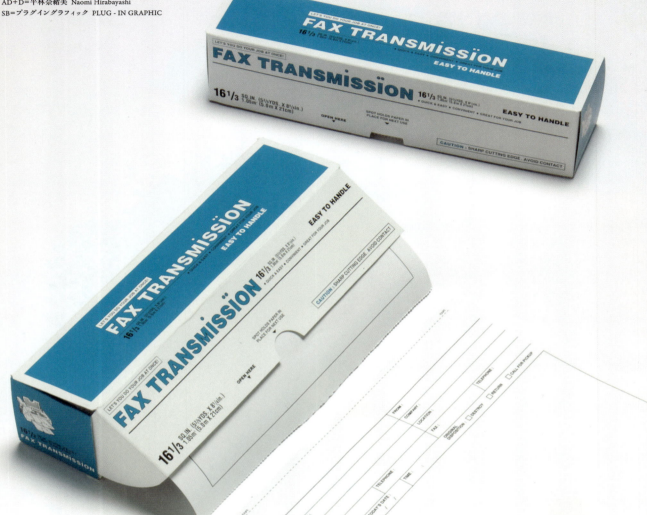

148

使いやすい食品用ラップタイプの
FAX送信用紙

食品用ラップやアルミホイルのように筒状で紙箱に収められ、
1回分ずつカットして使うファックス送信用紙。処理が簡単で、
手軽に使いやすくなっている。

Easy-to-use, kitchen
wrap-like fax paper

Fax paper in a roll that comes in a box and is used by cutting the
amount required each time, just like kitchen wrap or aluminum
foil. Neat, handy, and easy to use.

原稿用紙
Writing Paper
製紙メーカー Paper Manufacturer │ Japan

CL=竹尾 TAKEO Co., Ltd.
AD=水野 学 Manabu Mizuno
D=古屋貴広 Takahiro Furuya
DF=グッドデザインカンパニー good design company
SB=グッドデザインカンパニー good design company Co., Ltd.

プロダクト Product

失敗したら丸めて
地球儀や脳みそとして
ゴミ箱へ捨てられる原稿用紙

コクヨを仮想のクライアントとして提案。
失敗した原稿用紙を丸めてゴミ箱に捨てるという
作業から発想し、原稿用紙の裏面に
バスケットボールや地球儀、脳みその表面を印刷した。
紙の素性を効果的に生かす新しい提案として、
展示会に出品された。

Writing paper than can be crumpled into a ball and shot at a trash can basketball-style if a mistake is made

Taking a hint from the practice of crumpling up writing paper on which a mistake has been made and throwing it into a trash can, this product consists of notepaper with a basketball design, globe and the brains printed on the back. It was displayed in an exhibition as an example of a fresh idea that makes effective use of the characteristics of paper.

封筒
Enverope
製紙メーカー Paper Manufacturer │ Japan

CL=竹尾 TAKEO Co., Ltd.
AD=水野 学 Manabu Mizuno
D=古屋貴広 Takahiro Furuya
DF=グッドデザインカンパニー good design company
SB=グッドデザインカンパニー good design campany Co., Ltd.

はがき感覚で
立体物も送れる封筒

日本郵政公社を仮想のクライアントとし、
郵政民営化にともなった新しい封筒の
提案として2006年に製紙メーカー竹尾の
展示会に出展された。シート状の封筒を
折って四面体にし、立体物を送ることができる。

An envelope that enables 3D objects to be mailed in much the same way as a postcard

Exhibited at the 2006 Takeo Paper Show as a new kind of envelope to coincide with the privatization of Japan's postal service with Japan Post as the hypothetical client. The envelope is in the form of a sheet that can be folded into a tetrahedron and used to mail 3D objects.

紙エプロン パピエプ
Paper Epron papiepu

出版 Publishing | Japan

CL=京阪神エルマガジン社 L-magazine co., ltd.
AD+D=荻田 純 Jun Ogita
AD+D=古川智基 Tomoki Furukawa
P=岡田久仁子 Kuniko Okada
Stylist=東ゆうな Yuna Higashi
DF=サファリ SAFARI inc.
SB=サファリ SAFARI inc.

プロダクト Product

ファッション性あふれる、
おしゃれな紙エプロン

雑誌の付録として制作。〝焼肉や、カレーうどんを
食べるときにもっと洒落たペーパーエプロンを
つけたい!〟という会話からアイデアが生まれた。
つけ心地を考慮して柔らかい不織布を使用し、
オフセット印刷した。

A stylish paper apron created to make people aware of the possibilities of paper

Produced as a magazine project. The idea arose out of a
conversation during which someone commented, 'I want
to wear a more stylish paper apron when eating yakiniku
or curry udon.' Offset printed on soft, nonwoven fabric
out of consideration for the comfort of the wearer.

マジョリカ マジョルカ プレスキット
MAJOLICA MAJORCA Press Kit

化粧品メーカー Cosmetic Manufacturer | Japan

CL+SB=資生堂 Shiseido Co., Ltd.
CD+CW=吉田聖子 Shoko Yoshida
AD+D=大谷有紀 Yuki Otani

宝石箱のイメージで
つくられた化粧品のプレスキット

女性誌エディター向けのマジョリカ マジョルカの新製品の
プレスキット。太陽・灼熱をテーマにキラキラと輝くような
宝石箱のイメージで制作。紙を使って形状にこだわった
プレスキットに仕上げた。

A press kit for a new cosmetics product produced based on an image of a jewel case

A press kit for a new MAJOLICA MAJORCA product aimed at
women's magazine editors. It was produced with a Sun/
incandescence theme based on an image of a glittering jewel
case. Paper was used to produce the press kit that was made to
resemble as closely as possible the shape of a jewel case.

ネピアティッシュ
NEPIA Tissue

製紙メーカー Paper Manufacturer | Japan

CL=竹尾 TAKEO Co., Ltd.
AD=水野 学 Manabu Mizuno
D=古屋貴広 Takahiro Furuya
DF=グッドデザインカンパニー good design company
SB=グッドデザインカンパニー good design company Co., Ltd.

透けて中身の分かるティッシュケース

王子ネピアを仮想のクライアントとし、
2006年の製紙メーカー竹尾のペーパーショウに出品された
ティッシュケース。半透明の紙を使用し、
ティッシュの残量がわかるようになっている。

A tissue case that's see-through so the owner can see the contents

A tissue case exhibited at the 2006 Takeo Paper Show with Oji Nepia as the hypothetical client. Translucent paper is used allowing the user to see how many tissues remain in the case.

Pandora ノートブック
Pandora Note Book

プロダクトブランド Product Brand｜Japan

CL＝ディーブロス D-BROS
CD＝宮田 識 Satoru Miyata
AD＋D＋I＝天宅 正 Masashi Tentaku
SB＝ドラフト DRAFT Co., Ltd.

プロダクト Product

動物が閉じ込められた檻の1本に ゴムを利用した楽しいノート

ページがばらけるのを防ぐ為についているゴム紐を、
動物が閉じ込められている檻の柵の1本に見立てたノート。
使用時にゴム紐を外すことによって、動物たちは檻から
自由に出ることができる。

A notebook that comes in three sizes depending on the animal locked in the cage

A notebook in which the elastic cords designed to prevent the pages
coming loose resemble the bars of a cage containing an animal. When
the notebook is in use, the elastic cords are removed enabling the
animals to roam free.

ギンザサローネ企画展作品
Art works for an exhibition GINZA SALONE

ギャラリー Gallery | Japan

CL=ギンザ グラフィック ギャラリー ginza graphic gallery
CD+AD+D=佐野研二郎 Kenjiro Sano
SB=MR_DESIGN

プロダクト　Product

アートディレクターの独自のデザイン論が見えてくるオリジナルグッズ

アートディレクター佐野研二郎の展覧会で発表された実際の商品化を
目的とした新作オリジナルグッズ。ショートケーキメモブロックや
バンドエイドポストイットなど様々な形のコミュニケーションを提案した。

Original merchandise that reflects the art director's own unique design philosophy

New original merchandise developed with the aim of
commercialization presented at an exhibition of works by art director
Kenjiro Sano. Various forms of communication were proposed,
including shortcake memo blocks and band-aid post-its.

転〝korogaru〟CD パッケージ
"Rolling" CD Package

バンド　Band｜Japan

CL＝ゆやゆよん YUYAYUYON
CD＋AD＋D＝池澤 樹 Tatsuki Ikezawa
CW＝上野靖弘 Yasuhiro Ueno
SB＝東急エージェンシー Tokyu Agency Inc.

プロダクト　Product

6枚で1つのさいころになる
CD パッケージ

インディーズバンドの6ヶ月連続リリースCDのパッケージ。
CDタイトルである〝転〟から〝さいころ〟をメインモチーフに採用し、
6ヶ月連続なので6枚で1個のパッケージになる仕組みにした。

Six CD packages that form a
die when combined

Packaging for a series of six CDs issued in as many months
by an indies rock band. Inspired the CD title, which means
'roll' in English, a die was chosen as the main motif and the
packaging designed so that the series of six could be
combined to form a single package in the shape of a die.

154

CL＋CD＋SB＝ファイナル ホーム　FANAL HOME
D＝津村耕佑　Kosuke Tsumura

155

避難食としてのチョコレートを モチーフにしたキャンドルとTシャツ

都市で災害が起こった際に必要なアイテムを提供するブランドの
商品。災害時に必須のキャンドルとTシャツを、チョコレートの
イメージで制作した。キャンドルは小分けにでき、状況に応じて炎を
増やすことができる。また、Tシャツは板チョコのように見せるため
真空パックの型を使って封入した。

Candles and T-shirts that make use of the same packaging design as chocolates and play up the gap between the packaging and the contents

In order to communicate the idea of survival in the city that also
happens to be the brand concept, the image of energy associated with
chocolates is transformed into candles, which are necessary for
survival. The candles can be used individually and the number of
flames increased depending on the circumstances.

お中元・お年賀グッズ
Gift-giving season (summer / New year's) items

制作会社 Production Firm｜Japan

CL+SB＝ウルトラ ULTRA inc.
CD＋PL＋CW＝松本博房 Hirofusa Matsumoto（c, d）
CD＋CW＝田中康嗣 Koji Tanaka（a, b, c）
D＋Planner＝トーノ Tono（c）
D＝シャーベット遠藤 Sherbet Endo（c）
D＋Planner＝吉岡賢一 Kenichi Yoshioka（b）
D＋Planner＝吉田三智子 Michiko Yoshida（a）
I＋D＋Planner＝山田幸栄 Yukie Yamada（d）
Planner＝小林直樹 Naoki Kobayashi（d）
Planner＝馬場亮太 Ryota Baba（a）
Planner＝田中司毅 Shiki Tanaka
Planner＝翠川亜紀子 Akiko Midorikawa

156

季節感と意外性をもとにつくられた
制作会社の顧客向けギフトグッズ

クロスメディア・エンターテインメントを企画制作する会社が
顧客に対し、日ごろの感謝・暑中見舞い・お年賀として制作した
様々なグッズ。新巻鮭やお面など、季節感と意外性をもとに
ほとんどが手作りされている。

Gifts for customers produced with an emphasis
on a sense of season and their wow factor

A range of items produced by crossmedia entertainment producer Ultra for use as
gifts for customers on various occasions throughout the year, including during
the summer and New Year gift-giving seasons. The gifts include salted salmon,
masks, and other items, most of which were created with an emphasis on a sense
of season and their wow factor.

Wrigley's Extra White 紙コップ
Wrigley's Extra White Paper Cup

製薬 Pharmaceuticals | Germany

CL＝Wrigley GMBH
CD＝Sebastian Hardiecr
CD＝Marie-Theres Schwingeler
AD＝Patrick Hahne
AD＝Milena Micschochs
AD＝Eva-Maria Schwingeler
AD＝Jan Buchhola
CW＝Elias Rouloures
P＝JUPITER IMAGES
SB＝BBDO Duesseldorf GMBH

テイクアウトのコーヒーカップを利用したチューインガムの広告

競合他社製品の広告がない場所での展開を狙った
チューインガムのプロモーションツール。
テイクアウトのコーヒーのカップの底に真っ白な
歯の笑顔のシールを貼り付けて、街中や地下鉄、
オフィスなどで歩く広告とした。

A chewing gum advertisement that employs a take-out coffee cup

A promotional tool for chewing gum designed for use in areas where there are no advertisements for rival companies' products. A seal of a dazzling white smile was attached to the bottom of a take out coffee cup and the gimmick deployed as a walking advertisement on the street, on the subway, and in offices.

ADVIL メモパッド
ADVIL Memo Pad

製薬 Pharmaceuticals | Philippines

CL＝(ADVIL) WYETH CONSUMER HEALTHCARE
CD＝Mervin Mangada
AD＝Louie Cale
P＝Neil Lucente
P＝Claudine Sia
CW＝Tanke Tankeko
Priting Director＝May Dalisay
Account Supervisor＝Portia Catwra
Account Supervisor＝Belay Santillan
SB＝TBWA \ Santiago Mangada Puno

痛みの元に直接効くことを表現した鎮痛剤の広告メモパッド

製品の信頼性、認知度を高めるために、痛みの元に
すぐ届くという長所を、ペンスタンドメモという日常的なものを
使い、直接的にインパクトのある方法で提示。
競合他社製品との差を打ち出した。

An advertising Memo Pad for a painkilling drug that demonstrates how it acts directly on the source of the pain

Shows directly using an everyday item in the form of a pen stand memo pad the benefits of a painkiller that acts quickly on the source of the pain in a way that has real impact, both highlighting the reliability of the product and increasing recognition levels. Spells out the difference between the product and competing brands.

AGIニューヴォイスブック
AGI New Voice Book

デザイン会社、出版 Design Firm , Publishing ｜ Germany

CL＝Alliance Graphique Internationale (AGI)
CD＋AD＋D＝Jianping He
P＝Phillip Birau (Berlin)
P＝Yi Man(Shenzhen)
DF＋SB＝hesign international

書籍
Book

〝ニューヴォイス（新しい声）〟から
連想して耳がついた年鑑本

国際グラフィック連盟（AGI）の新規会員の作品紹介と
会議報告書が掲載された年鑑。背の部分を糸で綴じた
伝統的な装丁を使用し、タイトルから連想した耳が
飛び出すような形のカッティングになっている。

A yearbook with an ear, an idea suggested by the volume's title (New Voice)

A yearbook published by the Alliance Graphique
Internationale (AGI) showcasing the work of new
members and containing reports of meetings. The spine
is bound with string using a traditional method and has
a cutout ear that sticks out, an idea suggested by the
volume's title.

158

職業体験ハンドブック
Work Experience Hand Book

パッケージブランド Packaging Brand ｜ UK

CL＝Somerset College of Arts and Technology
CD＋D＋I＝Ben Cox
DF＋SB＝Studio 6.3

手の形をした学生向けの職業体験ハンドブック

学生向けにアドバイスを与えることを目的とした職業体験
ハンドブック。本は手の形をしており、タイトルと本の用途を、
しゃれを利かし魅力的に表現している。

A work experience handbook for students in the shape of a hand

A work experience handbook aimed at offering advice to
students. The book is in the shape of a hand, making clever
use of a pun based on the book's title and its purpose.

Book End ブックカバー
Book End Book Cover

パッケージブランド Packaging Brand │ UK

CL＝2134 Books
CD＋D＝Ben Cox
DF＋SB＝Studio 6.3

〝ブックエンド〟と名づけられた
ブックエンドとして使用できる
ブックカバー

本を垂直に保つようデザインされたブックカバー。
このカバーを掛けた本はブックエンドとして機能する。
切り抜き、単色のボール紙、ニス塗り仕上げで
シンプルに制作した。サイズと色にはバリエーションがある。

A book cover that can also be used as a bookend

A book cover designed to keep the book inside standing vertically. A book with this cover attached can also be used as a bookend. The product is simply made from cutouts and single-color cardboard and is varnished. Comes in a variety of sizes and colors.

書籍 Book

夜、眠る前に読む本
A Book for reading at night before sleep

製紙メーカー Paper Manufacturer │ Japan

CL＝竹尾 TAKEO Co., Ltd.
AD＋D＝永松りょうこ Ryoko Nagamatsu

横になりながらでも読みやすい
上部にテキストがある本

〝夜、眠る前に読む本〟として、
展示会で新しい本の形態を提案した。
寝ながら本を読んでいるときに、ふと思いつき、
テキストレイアウトの位置をページ上部にした。

A book with the text at the top of the page, an idea that arose while the designer was reading in bed

An idea from an exhibition for new forms of books in the shape of 'a book for reading at night before sleeping.' The idea of changing the text layout position to the top of the page came to the designer while they were reading in bed.

ゴス展カタログ
Goth Exhibition Catalog

美術館 Art Museum │ Japan

CL＝横浜美術館 Yokohama Art Museum
AD＋D＝青木康子 Yasuko Aoki
DF＋SB＝パンゲア PANGAEA Ltd.

小口に見え隠れする文字とイメージで
人間の内面性を表現した
展覧会カタログ

GOTH という言葉の響きが持つ重さときらびやかさ、
見え隠れする人間の内面性を1冊の固まりとして表現。
ページをめくろうとすると小口に〝GOTH〟の文字が現れ、
表4からめくるとドクロと蜘蛛が現れる。

An exhibition catalog that expresses the inwardness
of human beings in the form of words and images
that appear and disappear on the edges of the pages

Expresses in a single volume the seriousness and gorgeousness associated with
the word "Goth" and the sometimes visible, sometimes invisible inwardness of
human beings. As one leafs through the catalog, the word "Goth" appears on
the edges of the pages, and if one thumbs the pages from the outside back cover
a skull and spider appear.

インデックス
Index

作品提供者リスト
Submitter list

国内／Japan

海外／Overseas

クライアントリスト
Client list

国内／Japan

海外／Overseas

ハートを掴む ベストアイデアグラフィックス
Ideas Unleashed
Exceptional Achievements in Graphic Design

Jacket Design
Art Director & Designer
谷一和志（博報堂）Kazushi Taniichi (HAKUHODO INC.)
Designer
谷本尚子（博報堂）Naoko Tanimoto (HAKUHODO INC.)

Art Director
柴 亜季子 Akiko Shiba

Designer
三木俊一 Shunichi Miki

Editor
山本章子 Akiko Yamamoto
西岡詠美 Emi Nishioka

Photographer
藤本邦治 Kuniharu Fujimoto

Writer
加藤 希 Nozomi Kato

Translator
パメラ・ミキ Pamela Miki

Publisher
三芳伸吾 Shingo Miyoshi

2008年7月8日　初版第1刷発行

PIE BOOKS
2-32-4, Minami-Otsuka, Toshima-ku, Tokyo 170-0005 Japan
tel : +81-3-5395-4811　fax : +81-3-5395-4812
e-mail: editor@piebooks.com　sales@piebooks.com
http://www.piebooks.com

発行所
ピエ・ブックス
170-0005 東京都豊島区南大塚2-32-4
編集　tel: 03-5395-4820　fax: 03-5395-4821
　　　e-mail: editor@piebooks.com
営業　tel: 03-5395-4811　fax: 03-5395-4812
　　　e-mail: sales@piebooks.com
　　　http://www.piebooks.com

印刷・製本
大日本印刷株式会社
株式会社日本美術ライト商会

IN-STORE DISPLAY GRAPHICS
店頭コミュニケーショングラフィックス

Page: 216 (Full Color)　￥14,000+Tax

店頭でのプロモーション展開においては、空間デザインだけでなくグラフィックデザインが果たす役割も重要です。本書では、空間のイメージとグラフィックツールのコンセプトが一貫している作品をはじめ、限られたスペースで有効活用できるディスプレーキットや、P.O.P. の役割も果たすショップツールなどを広く紹介します。

A useful display tool for a limited space, display examples which show the harmonization among packaging, shop interior and in-store promotional graphics, a creative point-of-sale tool which stands out among others. This book is a perfect resource for designers and marketing professionals.

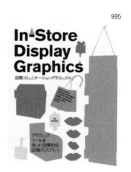

995

CHARACTER DESIGN TODAY
キャラクターデザイン・トゥデイ

Page: 232 (Full Color)　￥14,000+Tax

キャラクターは企業と消費者とを結ぶ有効なコミュニケーションツールといえます。競合商品との差別化をはかるため、企業のサービスを消費者にわかりやすく伝えるためなど、その役割は様々です。本書では、キャラクターのデザインコンセプト、プロフィールとともに広告やツールの展開例を収録。巻頭では、キャラクターが決定するまでの過程やボツ案を特集し、長く愛されるキャラクターをデザインするポイントを探ります。

200 successful characters with each profile, concept as well as the graphic examples. A featured article about the process of creating a character from scratch is also included with useful examples.

984

PACKAGE FORM AND DESIGN
ペーパーパッケージデザイン大全集　作例＆展開図(CD-ROM付)

Page: 240 (Full Color)　￥7,800+Tax

大好評の折り方シリーズ第3弾。製品を守りブランドアイデンティティーのアピールとなるパッケージ。本書ではバラエティーに富んだかたちのペーパーパッケージ約200点を国内外から集め、その作例と展開図を紹介していきます。展開図を掲載したCD-ROM付きでクリエイターやパッケージ制作に関わる人たちの参考資料として永久保存版の1冊です。

This is the third title focusing on paper packaging in "Encyclopedia of Paper Folding Design" series. The 150 high quality works are all created by the industry professionals; the perfect shapes and beautiful designs are practical and yet artistic. The template files in pdf file on CD-ROM.

941

DESIGN IDEAS FOR RENEWAL
再生グラフィックス

Page: 240 (Full Color)　￥14,000+Tax

本書では "再生" をキーワードにデザインの力で既存の商業地や施設、ブランドを甦らせた事例を特集します。リニューアル後のグラフィックツールを中心に、デザインコンセプトや再生後の効果についても紹介します。企業や地域の魅力を再活性させるためにデザインが果たした役割を実感できる1冊です。

A collection of case studies - with "regeneration" and "renewal" as their keywords - showing commercial districts, facilities and brands brought back to life through the power of design. Focusing on mainly the post-renovation graphic tools, we present the design concepts and their regenerative effects through which readers will see the role that design can play in reigniting the allure of companies and communities.

977

GIRLY GRAPHICS
ガーリー グラフィックス

Page: 200 (Full Color)　￥9,800+Tax

"ガーリー" とは女の子らしさの見直しや、ポップでありながらもキュートといった、女の子らしさを楽しむポジティブな姿勢を意味します。そんな "ガーリー" な空気感を、ポスター・DM・カタログ・パッケージなどのデザイン領域で、魅力的に表現した作品を紹介します。

A word "girly" represents an expression of reconstructing positive images about being girls. Today, those powerful and contagious "girly" images with great impact successfully grab attentions not only from girls but also from a broad range of audience. This book features about those 300 enchanted and fascinated advertisements such as posters, catalogs, shop cards, business cards, books, CD jackets, greeting cards, letterheads, product packages and more.

1009

NEO JAPANESQUE DESIGN
ネオ ジャパネスク デザイン

Page: 224 (Full Color)　￥14,000+Tax

2006年2月に発刊し好評を得た「ネオ ジャパネスク グラフィックス」。待望の第二弾「ネオ ジャパネスク デザイン」がいよいよ登場。ショップイメージ・ロゴ＆マークのカテゴリが新たに加わり、内容・クオリティともにバージョンアップした "和" デザインの最前線を紹介します。

This is the sister edition to "Neo Japanesque Graphics" published in 2006, and this new book includes even more modern yet Japanese taste designs which will give creative professionals inspirational ideas for their projects. Among various graphic works, this second title features shop design such as restaurants, bars and hotels, also features a variety of Japanese logos.

996

文字を読ませる広告デザイン 2

Page: 192 (Full Color)　￥9,800+Tax

パッと見た時に文字が目に入ってきて、しかも読みやすいデザインの広告物やパッケージの特集です。優れたデザインや文字組み、コピーによって見る側に文字・文章を読ませることを第一に考えられた広告を厳選します。ポスター、新聞広告、チラシ、車内吊り、雑誌広告、DM、カタログ、パンフレット、本の装丁、パッケージ、看板・サインなど多岐なジャンルにわたり紹介します。

Sales in Japan only.

934

FASHION BRAND GRAPHICS
ファッション グラフィックス

Page: 160 (Full Color)　￥7,800+Tax

本書は、ファッション、アパレルにおけるグラフィックデザインに力を入れた販促ツールを、厳選して紹介します。通常のショップツールはもちろん、シーズンごと、キャンペーンごとのツールも掲載。激しく移り変わるファッション業界において、お客様を飽きさせない、華やかで魅力的な作品を凝縮した1冊です。

The fashion brands that appear in this collection are among the most highly regarded in Japan and herein we introduce some of their commonly used marketing tools including catalogues, shopping cards and shopping bags, together with their seasonal promotional tools and novelties. This publication serves for not only graphic designers, but also people in the fashion industry, marketing professionals.

962

GRAPHIC SIMPLICITY

シンプル グラフィックス

Page: 248 (Full Color)　¥14,000+Tax

上質でシンプルなデザイン — 見た目がすっきりとして美しいのはもちろんのこと、シンプルなのに個性的な作品、カラフルなのに上品な作品、フォントやロゴがさりげなく効いている作品など、その洗練されたデザインは見る人を魅了してやみません。本書は厳選された作品を国内外から集め、落ち着いた大人の雰囲気にまとめ上げた本物志向のグラフィックコレクションです。

973

Simple, high-quality design work: not just crisply elegant and eye catching, but uncluttered yet distinctive, colorful yet refined, making subtly effective use of fonts and logos; in short, sophisticated design that seduces all who sees it.

1&2 COLOR EDITORIAL DESIGN

１・２色でみせるエディトリアルデザイン

Page: 160 (Full Color)　¥7,800+Tax

少ない色数でエディトリアルデザインする際には、写真の表現や本文使用色に制限がある分、レイアウトや使用する紙に工夫や表現力が問われます。本書は1色、2色で魅力的にレイアウトされた作品を、インクや用紙データのスペックと併せて紹介します。

956

This book presents many of well-selected editorial design examples, featuring unique and outstanding works using one or two colors. All works in this single volume present designers enormous hints for effective and unique techniques with information on specs of inks and papers. Examples include PR pamphlets, magazines, catalogs, company brochures, and books.

PICTGRAM & ICON GRAPHICS 2

ピクトグラム＆アイコングラフィックス 2

Page: 208 (Full Color)　¥13,000+Tax

本書では、視覚化に成功した国内・海外のピクトグラムとアイコンを紹介します。空港・鉄道・病院・デパート・動物園といった施設の案内サインとして使用されているピクトグラムやマップ・フロアガイドをはじめ、雑誌やカタログの中で使用されているアイコンなど、身近なグラフィックまでを業種別に掲載。巻末に、一般的によく使われるピクトグラム（トイレ・エスカレーター・駐車場など）の種別一覧表を収録。

935

Second volume of the best-seller title "Pictogram and Icon Graphics". Full-loaded with the latest pictograms around the world. Signage, floor guides and maps in airport, railway, hospital, department store, zoo and many more. Contained a wide variety of icons, including those found in catalogs and magazines, etc.

BEST FLYER 365DAYS NEWSPAPER INSERT EDITION

ベストチラシ 365 デイズ　折込チラシ編

Page: 256 (Full Color)　¥14,000+Tax

一番身近な広告媒体である新聞の折込チラシ。地域に密着したお得な情報を提供するものから、セレブ＆クールで夢のようなビジュアルのものまで多種多様です。本書では、1年間（365日）の各セールスシーズンでまとめたものから、1枚だけで効果的に商品をPRしたチラシまで、優れたデザインの旬な折込チラシ800点を収録しています。広告の制作に携わる人びとに必携のデザインサンプル集です。

936

This book contains many examples of excellently designed, topical flyers, ranging from seasonal advertisements to flyers for a single product. It is an anthology of design samples for creative professionals in the advertising industry.

BEYOND ADVERTISING: COMMUNICATION DESIGN

コミュニケーション デザイン

Page: 224 (Full Color)　¥15,000+Tax

限られた予算のなか、ターゲットへ確実に届く、費用対効果の高い広告をどのように実現するか？ 今デザイナーには、広告デザインだけでなく、コミュニケーション方法までもデザインすることが求められています。本書では「消費者との新しいコミュニケーションのカタチ」をテーマに実施されたキャンペーンの事例を幅広く紹介。様々なキャンペーンを通して、コミュニケーションを成功させるヒントを探求します。

948

Reaching the target market a limited budget: how is cost effective promotion achieved? What are the most effective ways to combine print and digital media? What expression reaches the target market? The answers lie in this book, with "new ways and forms of communicating with the consumer" as its concept.

WORLD CALENDAR DESIGN

ワールドカレンダーデザイン

Page: 224 (Full Color)　¥9,800+Tax

本書では国内外のクリエーターから集めたカレンダーを特集します。優れたグラフィックスが楽しめるスタンダードなタイプから、形状のユニークなもの、仕掛けのあるものなど、形状別にカテゴリーに分けて紹介します。カレンダー制作のデザインソースとしてはもちろん、ユニークな作品を通じて、様々なグラフィックスに活かせるアイデアが実感できる内容です。

949

The newest and most distinctive calendars from designers around the world. The collection features a variety of calendar types highly selected from numerous outstanding works ranging from standard wall calendars to unique pieces in form and design, including lift-the flap calendar, 3D calendar, pencil calendar and more.

カタログ・新刊のご案内について

総合カタログ、新刊案内をご希望の方は、はさみ込みのアンケートはがきをご返送いただくか、下記ピエ・ブックスへご連絡下さい。

CATALOGS and INFORMATION ON NEW PUBLICATIONS

If you would like to receive a free copy of our general catalog or details of our new publications, please fill out the enclosed postcard and return it to us by mail or fax.

CATALOGUES ET INFORMATIONS SUR LES NOUVELLES PUBLICATIONS

Si vous désirez recevoir un exemplaire qratuit de notre catalogue généralou des détails sur nos nouvelles publication. veuillez compléter la carte réponse incluse et nous la retourner par courrierou par fax.

CATALOGE und INFORMATIONEN ÜBER NEUE TITLE

Wenn Sie unseren Gesamtkatalog oder Detailinformationen über unsere neuen Titel wünschen.fullen Sie bitte die beigefügte Postkarte aus und schicken Sie sie uns per Post oder Fax.

ピエ・ブックス

〒170-0005　東京都豊島区南大塚2-32-4
TEL: 03-5395-4811　FAX: 03-5395-4812
www.piebooks.com

PIE BOOKS

2-32-4 Minami-Otsuka Toshima-ku Tokyo 170-0005 JAPAN
TEL：+81-3-5395-4811 FAX：+81-3-5395-4812
www.piebooks.com